The Little Black Book of
BUSINESS
WORDS

D0877834

The Little Black Book of
BUSINESS
WORDS

Michael C. Thomsett

amacom

American Management Association

This book is available at a special
discount when ordered in bulk quantities.
For information, contact Special Sales Department,
AMACOM, a division of American Management Association,
135 West 50th Street, New York, NY 10020.

This publication is designed to provide accurate and authoritative
information in regard to the subject matter covered. It is sold with the
understanding that the publisher is not engaged in rendering legal,
accounting, or other professional service. If legal advice or other
expert assistance is required, the services of a competent professional
person should be sought.

Library of Congress Cataloging-in-Publication Data

Thomsett, Michael C.
    The little black book of business words / Michael C. Thomsett.
       p.   cm.
   ISBN 0-8144-7753-4 (pbk.)
    1. Business—Dictionaries. I. Title.
  HF1001.T46   1991
  650'.03—dc20   91-53061
                                              CIP

© 1991 Michael C. Thomsett.
All rights reserved.
Printed in the United States of America.

This publication may not be reproduced,
stored in a retrieval system,
or transmitted in whole or in part,
in any form or by any means, electronic,
mechanical, photocopying, recording, or otherwise,
without the prior written permission of AMACOM,
a division of American Management Association,
135 West 50th Street, New York, NY 10020.

Printing number

10 9 8 7 6 5 4

Preface

No language is simple, and the language of business may be one of the most complex of all. Certain terms and expressions have a number of different meanings, depending on the circumstances, the company, and even the department.

Everyone in business is required to master an ever-growing number of terms. Some are jargon unique to the company and characteristic of the culture in force. Other terms and expressions are commonly used; many have a number of different meanings. This Little Black Book suggests some common and basic meanings to the language of business, notably in the following areas:

Accounting
Automation
Bookkeeping
Finance
Human Resources
Insurance
Law
Marketing and Sales
Math

No one book can comprehensively offer every term used in business. Terminology is constantly evolving. I have avoided listing widely used and commonly understood words in the interest of space. Although some basic concepts and ideas are included in the following pages, this book is aimed at the middle-level manager interested in using a single book as a resource for terminology.

The Little Black Book series is a collection of books that summarize specific, practical ideas for the manager. This dictionary sums up many of the areas covered in previous books, and provides easy-to-find definitions for many of the terms discussed elsewhere in the series.

The Little Black Book of BUSINESS WORDS

A

abandonment   The voluntary disposal or donation of property, specifically business assets. Upon abandonment, any remaining book value of the asset is written off as a loss. In some instances, it is more economical to abandon property than to salvage it or try to sell it.

Example: Certain inventories owned by a corporation were damaged by weather. The value of the goods was so low that the costs involved in selling them would not justify the effort, so the company abandoned them. A book entry was made to record the elimination of what was then considered worthless assets.

ABC method   A system of assigning priority value to inventory items. The most expensive items are classified in the A group, while the least expensive are coded as C items. The designation may be used to reorganize placement in a storage facility or to determine the frequency of physical counts. Classifying inventory in this manner also helps companies to identify inventory purchasing trends from one season to another and to eliminate working capital problems associated with overpurchase of expensive items during lower-volume periods.

ability to pay   **1.** A theory of compensation policy stating that wage and salary levels should be based on a company's ability to pay for labor. Accordingly, compensation of employees should increase as profits increase. Supporters of this theory rarely suggest that, as profits diminish, compensation should be reduced as well. **2.** A theory of taxation stating that wealthy taxpayers should be expected to carry a larger tax burden than poorer ones; that income tax liabilities should be based on the ability to afford the tax. The theory

1

is difficult to apply, however, since overtaxation tends to diminish the relationship between wealth and ability to pay. Tax incentives become economic factors that affect the health of the economy, so the theory does not always work as well as it should.

absenteeism (Also known as *absence rate*) The rate of employees' absence from work. A rate greater than 5 percent is considered high. As absenteeism rises, management should see the trend as a sign of poor morale and a decline in internal motivation. Supervisors may track absenteeism as one measure of employee performance, as a basis for salary and merit increases, and to select employees for possible promotions and sharing of greater responsibility and authority.

absolute liability (Also called *liability without regard to fault* or *strict liability*) A form of liability without actual fault or without the requirement of intent. For example, a manufacturer can incur liability for a defective product even when there is no negligence or fault. The liability arises from the fact that the product is defective, not from any wrongdoing on the part of the manufacturer.

accelerated cost recovery system (ACRS) A provision enacted as part of the Economic Recovery Tax Act of 1981, which set up more rapid write-off provisions for capital asset depreciation than were allowed previously. The older concepts of salvage value and useful life were replaced with a recovery life system determined by asset classes. The system was drastically revised with passage of the Tax Reform Act of 1986.

accelerated depreciation One of several methods for depreciating capital assets. The depreciation allowed in earlier years of the recovery period is greater than that allowed in later years. Under the accelerated cost recovery system, accelerated depreciation in certain class lives reverts to straight-line depreciation during the later years. The computation involves first figuring the straight-line rate and then increasing the amount by the percentage allowed. For example, in a certain recovery class, the first few years' depreciation is allowed at the rate of 175 percent. The first step: Compute the straight-line rate. The second step: Increase the straight-line rate by 175 percent.

Under a strict 175 percent system, the next year's allowance depreciation would be computed as follows: (1) Reduce the basis by depreciation claimed in the previous year; (2) compute the straight-line rate on the remainder; (3) multiply the straight-line rate by 175 percent. Continue the process until (a) the asset has been completely depreciated or (b) depreciation reverts to a prescribed straight-line basis under accelerated cost recovery system rules.

See straight-line depreciation.

acceptance The granting of consent to an offer in a contract that leads to binding terms on both sides. An offer may be accepted or countered. A counteroffer may then be accepted by the other side. In either case, upon acceptance, a contract is created. A contract may not exist until a meeting of the minds has been established. One critical condition necessary to recognize that a meeting of the minds exists is that offer and acceptance are completed.

access The retrieval of stored information within an automated system and the ease or convenience of the process. Access should be planned for ease of retrieval: Stored materials should be identified by department, contents, and disposal date; similar materials should be stored in or near the same location. When related materials are stored separately, a cross-referencing system should be included in or on the storage medium (box, disk, or fiche).

accessibility The ability of a physically challenged worker or candidate for work to approach, enter, and use an employer's facilities. Accessibility is an important element in the areas of physically-challenged workers' rights and related legislation requiring that the workplace be made accessible. Failure to provide accessibility to physically challenged candidates or workers could result in liability.

Example: A job opening is advertised, but the personnel office is accessible only by climbing seven steps. There is no wheelchair ramp. A candidate for the position is unable to approach, so a case is made against the company claiming discrimination and noncompliance with the law. As a remedy, the company could install facilities allowing for ease of access. (It could also have advertised a willingness to meet a physically challenged applicant in another location.)

account analysis In accounting, the audit or study of an account in the general ledger, in a subsidiary ledger, or in the records of another company or department to identify the sources and nature of the balance or to verify balances and their contents as claimed by another. An account analysis may uncover coding errors, point out the need for reversing journal entries (as in the case of an accrual from a prior period), identify or prevent instances of embezzlement or opportunities to embezzle funds, or simply verify the accuracy of account entries. Proper maintenance of a set of books includes recurring account analysis and documentation of each account's contents. It should be possible at any time to fully account for the balances in all asset, liability, and net worth accounts and to exercise appropriate controls over all income, cost, and expense accounts.

accounting cycle   The series of actions that take place within an accounting system. In the typical cycle, an initiating entry is generated by a source document. Recording, coding, and verification follow, and each entry is gradually reduced to a summarized version for each account. The cycle ends when the accounting year is summarized and balanced, the books are closed, closing adjustment entries are made, and final statements are drawn. The final internal statements may be subject to review by an external auditor; from that audit, final adjusting entries may be made.

accounting method   One of two generally used methods for keeping company books.

- Under the cash method, transactions are entered into the books only when cash changes hands. The benefit of the cash accounting method is its simplicity; the major disadvantage is that it does not account for income or expenses due but not yet received or paid. *See* cash accounting.
- Under the accrual method, income is booked in the month earned, and costs or expenses are booked in the month incurred. The benefit of the accrual method is its accuracy; the disadvantage is that it requires more work and a higher degree of bookkeeping skill to keep the books balanced and under control. *See* accrual accounting.

Accounting methods may also be distinguished by the method under which accruals are recognized for accounting and tax purposes.

- Under the percentage-of-completion accounting method, income and costs are booked according to the degree of completion on the job. Any income received in advance is deferred; and income not yet received to that point is accrued. Costs are handled in a similar manner. Money spent beyond a given completion percentage is deferred. Costs incurred but not paid, up to the completion percentage, are accrued. *See* percentage–of–completion accounting.

▪ Under completed contract accounting, no part of the income or costs on a job are recognized until the entire job has been completed. Although this is a simpler method, it also distorts the true picture. For example, when a very large job is 95 percent complete as of the end of the year, none of the income or costs involved appear in the books and records of the company. *See* completed contract accounting.

accounting rate of return A straightforward but less than accurate method for calculating the return from an investment. Yield is not discounted or compounded in consideration of the time involved, but is spread evenly, on a straight–line basis. An overall yield is annualized, without regard for when or how the yield was earned. Discounted rate of return, in comparison, is more accurate since it also allows for the time value of money. Compounded rates of return significantly change the average annual return.

Example: An organization invests a $1 million reserve in bonds and stocks. Three years later, the portfolio has earned $210,000. Under the accounting rate of return method, each year's activity averages $70,000 in yield, or 7 percent per year. Under the discounted rate of return method, the actual yield could be much higher or lower, depending on (a) the timing of earnings, (b) compounded return, if any, and (c) the timing of any capital gains or losses.

accounts payable The current debts of the organization due within the immediate future. Accounts payable generally includes money due to vendors and to providers of overhead–related services (such as telephone, utilities, maintenance, rent). An *account* payable is normally associated with recurring current debts of the organization that arise from one month to the next. In comparison, a *note* or *contract* payable more commonly is associated with a loan from a bank or other outside source. Another distinction is the timing of the due date. Accounts payable are almost always due within the next 12 months, so they are current liabilities. Notes and contracts payable may be partially due within the coming year, while another part of the liability is not. The second group represents long-term liabilities.

accounts receivable   Current asset representing amounts due to the organization from customers. As current assets, the balances are assumed to be convertible to cash within the coming 12 months. The amount of outstanding receivables may be reduced by a reserve for bad debts or an account with a similar name; the balance in this separate account is an estimate of receivables that will not be collected. *See* allowance for bad debts; bad debt.

When the volume is high and a large number of customers are involved each month, the company may control its accounts receivable records under an elaborate subsidiary system. Ideally, information reported in the general ledger should be highly summarized. Monthly entries should include one number for charges generated and one for cash received. The details of each are recorded in the subsidiary ledger, with a separate page or record for each customer. Upon balancing the subsidiary ledger at the end of each month, the sum of customer account balances should always equal the ending balance of accounts receivable in the general ledger.

accrual accounting   One of two accounting methods, the other being cash accounting. Under the accrual system, income entries are made to the books as amounts are earned; costs and expenses are entered as they are incurred. For example, a company may earn a large amount of income this month, but cash will not be received for 60 days. Under the accrual system, that income is recognized currently. Under the cash system, it is not recognized or booked until received.

The same rules are applied to costs and expenses. For example, a company might sign an agreement to receive several hundreds of dollars in supplies. Under the accrual system, that expense is incurred currently, and will be booked as an account payable. Under the cash system, the expense would not be acknowledged until the bill was paid. *See* cash accounting.

accumulated depreciation   An asset account that reduces the value of long-term or fixed assets. As depreciation entries are made periodically, the accumulated depreciation account is increased. This process continues until all allowed depreciation has been claimed. At that point, the accumulated depreciation account's balance will equal the asset value in the books. Accumulated depreciation is recognized by a noncash journal entry.

Example: At the end of the year, an asset is subject to depreciation. The company claims straight-line depreciation over a five-year period. The asset has a basis of $5,000, so annual depreciation is $1,000 per year. The depreciation expense account is debited $1,000 and the asset account, Accumulated Depreciation, is credited $1,000.

acquisition cost   The total cost of acquiring property besides the purchase price. For example, the stated purchase price of an asset might not include the entire acquisition cost, which may include interest, sales tax, registration fees, transportation, and other costs or expenses.

ACRS   *See* accelerated cost recovery system.

actual cash value (ACV)   A form of property and casualty insurance in which losses are paid not at replacement value, but at current value, less a calculated amount for depreciation, as figured by the insurance company. The depreciation is calculated based on the age of the items lost and an assumed useful life and replacement value. Unlike full replacement cost coverage, ACV insurance will not fully replace losses at today's market value.

address   The precise location of data stored in computer memory, represented by a numeric code.

adjusted basis   For accounting and tax purposes, the original cost of an asset, reduced by accumulated depreciation and increased by the value of capital improvements. Calculation of adjusted basis is necessary for computation of capital gain or loss upon sale of the asset. The adjusted purchase price, compared to the adjusted sales price, represents the amount of gain or loss.

Example: Real estate is purchased by a company for $400,000. Over a period of years, $182,000 is claimed in depreciation, and $106,000 in improvements are added. Adjusted basis is:

Original cost	$400,000
Less depreciation	− 182,000
Plus improvements	+ 106,000
Adjusted basis	$324,000

adjustment journal   A journal created to correct an error or to modify a value. Journals may be made for noncash entries (such as depreciation or amortization); for accruals and reversals of previous accruals; or to make adjustments. For example, an expense is entered to the wrong account and the error is not discovered until the following month. The adjustment journal entry is made to correct the error reflected in the previous period.

adverse impact   A method of selection in hiring, transfer, promotion, training, and other decisions of employment that is substantially different for certain people. Specific groups are defined as members of a race, ethnic group, or sex. If the selection rate is lower than 80 percent of the selection rate of the group with the highest rate of selection, then the selection method or rate is considered as having adverse impact. *See also* impact ratio.

adverse opinion   (also known as a *qualified opinion*)   The opinion expressed by an independent auditor concerning the accuracy and completeness of financial statements. In the auditor's opinion, the books and records and financial statements do *not* reflect true conditions or operations, or do *not* conform to generally accepted accounting and auditing standards. Such an opinion arises when certain transactions or balances cannot be verified due to shortcomings in the company's recordkeeping system or when the company's management disagrees with the auditor's findings and recommendations, and refuses to revalue, adjust, or correct the problem.

advertising allowance   A payment made to a merchant or other customer as compensation for advertising or promoting products. For example, a company wanting a merchant to emphasize its product may supply standing cardboard displays to be placed near the store's entrance and, as inducement to place them, offers a cash bonus or deep discount on the cost of items to be displayed.

advertising reserve   A budget fund or amount that has been set up in anticipation of future expenses, but without a specific breakdown of those expenses in mind; or created as a fund for contingencies.

    Example: A reserve is established in the amount of $700,000. No detailed assumptions or classifications are imposed on the advertising department. It is allowed to spend the money where it wants, and the only condition is that a budgeted level of response will be generated as a result.

    See also reserve.

affected class   An employee, former employee, or applicant or candidate for employment who has been denied employment or the benefits of employment as a result of discriminatory practices. To prove the existence of an affected class, three points must be established:

1. There is evidence of discrimination against the affected class.
2. There is evidence of the consequences or effects of discrimination.
3. Individuals who have suffered from that discrimination are identified.

affirmative action   Actions undertaken in hiring and employment practices to offset past abuses and discriminatory policies.

after-tax profit   The net profit earned after deducting an allowance for income taxes. In any discussion of *profit* or *net profit,* this clarification is an important one. In some usages or versions, the term *profit* does not allow for nonoperating income and expenses (such as capital gains or losses, cash overages and shortages, interest income and expense, or gain and loss from exchange fluctuation). In other instances, profit may be stated without deducting a provision for income taxes. The differences between operating profit and net profit may be significant. And the difference between pretax and after-tax profit may also be worth distinguishing, especially for the purpose of comparing results between two or more different companies. *See also* net income; operating profit; pretax profit.

agenda   A listing of issues, problems, and topics to be discussed during a business meeting. Agenda items may lead to assignments for action and execution, a decision for departmental action and deadline, or deferral for discussion at a later meeting.

The agenda is a critical tool for maintaining control of meetings. With a published agenda, the meeting leader may schedule and direct discussion to ensure that all topics to be covered *are* covered. Without a written agenda, the meeting may lack direction and cohesion.

aging list   A listing of accounts receivable shown by the age of the amount outstanding. One total column is broken down into categories, the most common being:

Current (zero to thirty days)
Thirty-one to sixty days
Sixty-one to ninety days
Past due

The aging list is a useful collection tool which, if used to monitor receivables, may help in collecting funds before they become past due. The longer accounts are allowed to remain unpaid, the greater the risk of bad debts. Thus, monitoring through simple procedures such as the aging list is worth the small analytical effort required.

allocation   The accounting practice of assigning income, costs, or expenses to divisions or departments. In cost accounting, allocation is often made on a very detailed basis. Costs and expenses may be broken down on the basis of the number of employees, square footage for a department, telephone hours, utility usage, or fixed monthly allowance. Expenses may be more difficult to break down on any but an arbitrary basis, since they may not be assignable directly to one job or department.

Allocation in nonproduction environments often leads to conflict or excessive work for accounting departments, notably during budget development and review. In such environments, where there are no direct costs, allocation of general expenses—especially those beyond the budgetary control of the department manager—provides nothing of value and reveals no trends to which anyone can react.

allowance for bad debts   A reduction of the accounts receivable asset to estimate near-future bad debt write-offs. The allowance may be a percentage of outstanding receivables or based on a historical trend. The purpose is to equalize and estimate bad debts over a period of months, rather than distorting the financial report in the one month where a bad debt is recognized.

allowed time (Also known as *standard time*)   The amount of time a task should require, based on measurement of standard performance for that task.

alpha   A field of information consisting only of alphabetical characters.

alternative hypothesis   In statistics, the assumptions and beliefs used by analysts to develop and set the standards of a probability study, in place of the standard, or null hypothesis. *See* null hypothesis.

amortization   The gradual write-off of an asset other than a tangible, fixed asset. Capital assets, such as buildings, furniture, fixtures, and equipment are subject to depreciation. Other assets, such as improvements to real property or intangible assets, are amortized. So are organizational costs, the asset value of covenants not to compete, and prepaid assets (such as prepaid insurance, rent, or interest). Amortization is not accumulated as an offset to an asset, however, as is depreciation. Rather, the asset is reduced directly in book value as an offset to the expense as it is booked.

amortization payments   Payments required to amortize, or pay off, a loan, such as a mortgage or a fully amortized business debt. The periodic payment is scheduled to retire the debt in a specified number of years, based on the interest rate, time, and compounding method being applied. The method of computation requires the following steps:

1. Divide the annual interest rate by 12, to arrive at the monthly rate.
2. Multiply the monthly rate by the previous balance of the loan. This is the interest for the current period.
3. Subtract the current period interest from the total payment due this month. The result is the principal.
4. Subtract the principal from the outstanding balance. The result is the new loan balance, to be carried forward to the following month.

annual compounding   A method of compounding in which interest is calculated once per year. This is distinguished from simple interest in the way that subsequent years' interest is calculated. Under the simple interest method, the same amount is paid or earned each year. With annual compounding, the first year's interest is added to principal, and the total earns interest the following year.

   Example: $1,000 yields 8 percent per year. Under simple interest, this is $80 each and every year. Under annual compounding, the amount is $80 the first year. The second year's interest is $86.40:

$$\$1,080 \times 8\% = \$86.40$$

The formula for calculating annual compounding involves multiplying the principal amount by the rate of interest (expressed in decimal form), for the number of years involved.

$$P \times r \times t = i$$

P = Principal t = Time
r = Rate i = Interest

See also compound interest; simple interest.

annual debt service   The amount of payments required during one full year, including both principal and interest, to continue timely payments on a debt. Annual debt service is an important piece of financial information when projecting cash flow, since principal payments might not be included when a schedule of interest is reviewed in isolation. The total of annual debt service represents a current liability for a company. The amount due above the annual debt service is considered a long-term liability.

annualized yield   The yield from an investment expressed in a uniform manner, regardless of varying holding periods.

Example: Four different investments each yield $100 in interest; but they are held for different periods of time. In order to make a valid comparison of investment value, (1) divide the total yield by the number of months the investment was held; (2) multiply the result by 12. The answer is the yield that would have been earned if the investment had been held for one year.

$$\frac{Y}{M} \times 12 = A$$

Y = Yield
M = Months held
A = Annualized yield

annual meeting   A meeting during which the management of a corporation presents a detailed summary and report of conditions and operations, to the stockholders. The board of directors may vote on shareholder resolutions, elect officers, or transact other important business.

annual percentage rate (APR)   The effective annual rate, including an allowance for compound interest. The APR will vary based on the method and frequency of compounding, with a greater difference at higher rates of interest.

   Example: When interest is paid at 6 percent, the APR for monthly compounding is 6.168 percent; and the APR for quarterly compounding is 6.136 percent.

   APR is calculated in a number of steps.

1. Divide the annual rate by the number of compound periods (12 for monthly and 4 for quarterly). This is the monthly rate.
2. Add 1 to the monthly rate.
3. Multiply it by itself for the number of compound periods.
4. Subtract 1.

The result is the APR in decimal form.

   Example: Using quarterly compounding at 6 percent, the steps are as follows:

$$\frac{0.06}{4} = 0.015$$

$$0.015 + 1 = 1.015$$

$$1.015 \times 1.015 \times 1.015 \times 1.015 = 1.06136$$

The annual percentage rate reflects the true annual cost or benefit of interest, based on the effects of compounding during the year.

   See also compound interest.

annual report   1. In accounting, the annual financial statement which meets disclosure requirements dictated by the Securities and Exchange Commission. The balance sheet, income statement, and statement of cash flows must be included, and the books and records must be audited by an independent external auditor. **2.** An expansion of the annual financial statement, which is packaged in a multicolor brochure sent to stockholders. The report includes audited financial statements as well as many pages of public relations material, aimed at encouraging investors to buy and hold stock in the corporation.

apparent authority   A concept in law stating that a principal is responsible for acts of an agent, when the principal suggests to someone else by way of statements or conduct that the agent speaks for the principal. That suggestion, while not specific, is the apparent authority that leads others to believe there is a principal/agent relationship.

application   A computer program created to serve a specific purpose, such as scheduling, accounts receivable, or budgeting.

APR   *See* annual percentage rate.

arbitration   The process of settling disagreements without resorting to litigation, or attempting to do so in the interest of avoiding litigation. An impartial umpire, or arbitrator, is appointed to hear both sides of the issue in a dispute. When both sides agree to be bound by the arbitrator's decision, it is referred to as binding arbitration. *See* mediation.

arm's-length transaction   Any commerce, action, or dealings between two or more parties, each acting in his or her own best interests. The distinction becomes important when dealings occur between certain parties, including husband-wife, parent-child, and corporation-subsidiary, which would not be arm's-length transactions. To qualify as an arm's length transaction, neither party may have a direct interest in the consequences or benefits of the outcome from the other point of view.

articles of incorporation   The document that spells out the terms of formation of a corporation, according to the domicile state laws.

ASCII   Acronym for American Standard Code for Information Interchange, a coding system in microcomputer processing used to store and transfer file contents.

asset   Something owned by a company and listed on the balance sheet. Offsetting the total value of assets are the combined values of liabilities and net worth. Balance sheet classifications include:

- *Current Assets.* Cash or assets convertible to cash within one year, including inventories, accounts receivable, notes receivable, and marketable securities.
- *Long-term Assets.* Also called fixed assets, the net value of capital assets, such as furniture, fixtures, equipment, machinery, and real estate. The basis of each asset is reduced by allowable depreciation.
- *Prepaid or Deferred Assets.* Assets representing expenditures applicable to a future period, or applicable over several periods. They are held as assets until the appropriate time, and then reversed; or they are amortized over the applicable term.
- *Intangible Assets.* Assets placed on the books without a corresponding cash transaction, such as goodwill, which represents the assumed value of the company's good name and reputation.

assignment   The transfer of rights to another, or appointment of another person as a representative in a fiduciary situation. For example, a lender may be given assignment as beneficiary under a life insurance policy as collateral for a loan. The cash value is assigned to the lender.

assumption base   The belief or series of beliefs that are used to support a budget or forecast. For example, a telephone budget may be developed on the assumption base that last year's average per employee is an accurate method for budgeting. Accordingly, the following year's budget is increased by the number of additional employees the manager plans to hire. In a sales forecast, assumption bases may include beliefs concerning the market, the expansion plan, the sales force, or recruitment and attrition trends.

attitude study   A survey of customers, the public, or a demographic group to determine attitudes toward a company's product or service, or toward the organization itself.

audience profile   A summary or report detailing the attributes, attitudes, or characteristics of the customer audience for a particular product or service. It may include average age, family size, residential area, and income.

audit   An examination of the books and records of a company or a department. Procedures as well as records are checked. For example, auditors may examine cash control procedures and recommend changes to better protect the company's liquid assets. The purpose of the audit is to suggest changes in procedures; to verify and qualify that the financial statements are accurate and complete; and to find and correct errors in procedures and in statements.

audit program   The series of steps taken during an audit, listed in detail. The auditor follows each of the steps and, working with the company's representative, determines along the way whether any material errors exist. Each step in the audit program is carefully summarized and cross-referenced on worksheets and placed into an audit file for review and approval by the senior auditor.

audit trail   The series of documents and entries in the books and records that prove a transaction or series of transactions. The audit trail usually begins with a source document, such as a receipt, a voucher, an invoice, or other original proof or verification. The final stage is the entry in the general ledger. A complete trail allows an auditor to trace any entry from source document, through the journals, to the ledger.

authoritarian leadership   Descriptive of a leader whose personality and style include an actively strong and directive role. Such a leader is involved in forming departmental or group activities, setting goals, and planning. However, the leader also tends to neither delegate well nor trust others with shared authority.

autocratic leadership   Descriptive of a leader who emphasizes task orientation but is unable to appreciate or acknowledge the importance of human relationships within a group. Such a leader is seen by others as lacking confidence, being unable to inspire, and disinterested in people.

B

back-up file A copy created to protect against losing information in case a file is erased or a disk is erased or damaged.

bad debt A debt that is considered uncollectible and, accordingly, is written off as a loss. Bad debts can be written off as an expense only when reporting on the accrual basis, when that debt was reported as income during a previous accounting period.

There are two general methods used for recording bad debts. One is through a reserve account. A calculated monthly average is deducted from the current asset for Accounts Receivable and written off each month. The reserve level is based on experience and is modified from time to time. The other method is to write off a specific bad debt only when it becomes worthless. While this method is more accurate, it also tends to distort the reporting of financial information over time. A good case can be made for the reserve method, since a partial bad debt is recognized each month. *See also* allowance for bad debts; reserve; write-off.

balance sheet A summary of assets, liabilities, and net worth as of the end of a period. The balance sheet is so called for a number of reasons.

- It shows the balances in each asset, liability, and net worth account.
- Double-entry records balance when the closing of income, cost, and expense accounts balance with the profit account as part of net worth.
- The sum of all assets must balance with the sum of liabilities plus net worth.

17

The first section is assets, broken down into current, long-term, prepaid or deferred, and intangible. The second group is liabilities, including current, long-term, and deferred credits. Finally, net worth includes capital stock, paid-in surplus, and retained earnings (in a corporation); or owner's equity net of draws, and a profit or loss account (in a partnership or sole proprietorship). The sum of liabilities and net worth is always equal to total assets.

BAP   *See* business automobile policy.

bar graph   A form of graph that compares relative values rather than values moving over a period of time, as in a line graph. For example, sales results for an entire year may be compared between actual and forecast, between divisions or from year to year. Bar graphs may be vertical or horizontal, the choice being a matter of readability, appearance, or fit. *See* line graph.

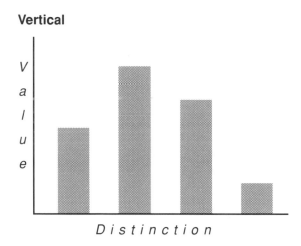

Vertical

Horizontal

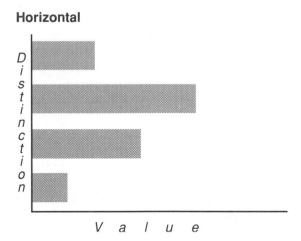

BASIC   Acronym for Beginners All-purpose Symbolic Instruction
   Code, a computer language developed in the 1960s for business and
   math programming.
baud   A term meaning "bits per second," representing the speed at
   which information moves through modems and other communications channels.
benefit formula   A method of calculating benefits in a group retirement plan. The result of the formula used will determine the
   amount of monthly payment each participant will receive. The
   formula may be based on a combination of age, years of service,
   and salary level.
bilateral contract   A contract in which both sides have equal consideration. When equal consideration is not granted, the contract and
   agreement for performance are unilateral.
billing cycle   The cycle from ordering of goods to receipt of a bill. In
   most instances, this cycle occurs monthly. A cut-off date for each
   supplier tells which bills will be on the current statement and which
   ones will show up the following month.
       Example: One vendor enforces a cut-off date of the 25th. A
   month-end statement shows all orders in the billing cycle occurring

between the 26th of the previous month and the 25th of the current
month.

binary   A system of numbering containing only two numerals, zero
and one. Information is stored and processed in computers in binary
form.

bit   Acronym for binary digit, a zero or a one in the storage system of
the computer.

blanket contract   Insurance in a single policy that provides multiple
coverage. Examples include group insurance offered as an employee
benefit or coverage of a company's inventory, stored in several
different locations but insured under a single policy.

blended rate   The average rate of two or more different loans or yields.
It may apply in a number of circumstances.

   Example: A lender wanting a borrower to refinance an existing
loan offers the holder of that long-term loan a rate that is greater
than that on the current loan but lower than prevailing market rates.

   Example: A borrower has two outstanding loans to one lender.
The combined payment made on the two loans is a blended rate
representing the weighted average between the two interest rates. It
will be weighted based on differences between principal or loan
amounts, with greater weight being given to rates on higher
amounts outstanding.

blind product test   A form of testing in which the participants are
asked to judge and compare products without knowledge of the
brand names or manufacturers.

books of final entry   The general ledger of a business, so called
because it is the end of the line that starts with a source document,
moves through the system of journals (books of original entry), and
ends up in highly summarized form.

books of original entry   The journals in a company's system of
books, including cash receipts, disbursements, and general journal,
along with any subsidiary records and journals.

book value   The value of stock based not on current market price, but
actual tangible net worth. To compute, (1) subtract intangible assets
from net worth; (2) divide by the number of shares of common
stock outstanding. The result is the book value per share.

$$\frac{N - I}{S} = B$$

N = Net worth
I = Intangible assets
S = Common stocks outstanding
B = Book value per share

BOP   *See* business owner's policy.
bottom   The support level of stocks or commodities, an economic cycle, or a market price of any type. When prices fall below an identified bottom, a new bottom is established. When prices stop falling and begin to rise, they are said to have bottomed out.
bottom line   Specifically, the amount of profit or loss as reported on the income statement. The term may often be used to identify the amount of profit after all nonoperating income and expenses have been taken into consideration and all taxes paid.

Generally, the term is used to distinguish between vague requests or statements and the issue that really counts.

Example: An employee gives a supervisor a number of observations or complaints. However, when asked to get to the "bottom line," the employee may state the specific request he or she has in mind.
brand   A line of products by a manufacturer distinguished from similar products from other manufacturers by symbols, words, or color combinations.
brand loyalty   The tendency of customers to continue using one brand over another.
break-even analysis   A determination of the volume of sales required to cover expenses. The analysis involves comparisons between fixed and variable costs and expenses.

Example: If direct costs are 45 percent and a company's fixed overhead is $125,000 per month, the break-even point is calculated at a dollar amount required to cover both costs and fixed overhead:

1. Subtract the percentage of direct costs from 100:

$$100 - 0.45 = 0.55$$

2. Divide fixed overhead by the answer to step 1:

$$\frac{125,000}{0.55} = 227,273$$

The result of this calculation is the dollar amount required to break even. This can be proven with a simple reversal of the test:

Sales	$227,273
Less: direct costs, 45 percent	102,273
Gross profit, 55 percent	$125,000
Less: fixed overhead	125,000
Profit or loss	$ 0

break-even point   The amount of sales necessary to cover expenses. This assumes certain factors concerning direct costs and expenses. For example, if either the cost or expense factors vary due to a change in sales volume, then the break-even point has to change as well. This is a likely event, as expenses tend to increase when increased volume periods are not accompanied by continued or increased controls over general expenses. When those controls do work, the break-even point may be lower than expected given the fixed nature of many expenses. Gross profit margins may also tend to fall as volume increases. The volume itself may be the result of lowered mark-up on products. The consequence may be a higher dollar value of gross profit with a substantially smaller percentage of gross margin.

bridge loan (also known as a *swing loan* or *gap financing*)   A temporary loan made in expectation of more permanent, long-term financing. For example, a company is given a bridge loan to fund initial construction of a new building, while it is obtaining licenses and taking bids. However, upon accepting a bid and getting the go-ahead, the company replaces the bridge loan with a bond issue or construction financing.

budget   A summary of the costs and expenses a company or department expects to realize during the coming year, six months, or other period. The budget may be prepared as part of an ongoing internal system of controls, or as part of a business and marketing plan.

budgeting The process of estimating the likely income, expenses, and cash flow of a business or department. Forecasts are made of sales, costs and expenses, and cash flow.

buffer A temporary storage area for a body of computer data for relatively rapid processing. It is used during printing routines, for example.

bug An error, usually in a software program, which prevents correct processing, storage, or retrieval of information.

bureaucratic leadership A style of leadership that emphasizes procedures and historical methods, even when those methods are no longer working. The tendency is to attempt to solve current problems by adding layers of control, forms, or time-consuming procedures.

business automobile policy (BAP) An insurance policy providing protection against a variety of losses connected to the business use of an automobile. The policy includes geographic limits, types of casualties and liabilities covered, ceilings on the amount of protection, and specific limitations concerning who may drive the automobile. In addition, the policy provides coverage only while the automobile is being used for business purposes.

business cycle **1.** The identifiable period of activity of a given company during certain parts of the year; or the pattern of higher or lower than average activity during certain months. **2.** In some applications, the business cycle is used to mean the monthly cycle in accounting. **3.** A term describing national inflationary, recessionary, and other trends in the economy.

business liability Insurance protection against one or more damages resulting from the operation of a business. Insurance may be in the form of direct liability coverage (covering actions of employees or the condition of products, for example); or contingent liability (possible damages occurring in the future). *See also* liability insurance.

business necessity A concept that an otherwise unacceptable or discriminatory business practice is acceptable upon proof of two points:

1. The practice is necessary for reasons of safety or efficiency in the work environment.
2. There is no reasonable alternative to solve the problem that would have less impact.

business owner's policy (BOP)   Insurance especially designed for the small business owner. Protection extends to losses from bodily injury on the business premises, with restrictions on how many people may be present at one time. Certain types of businesses or uses of the property may be excluded from the coverage.

business planning   The process of mapping out the likely or possible future. The planning process should coordinate marketing expansion with the broader and longer-term directions established by top management. The document produced from the process should include complete forecasts and budgets for at least one year. Some companies attempt to indicate general directions through the budgeting process for up to five years. Business planning is helpful in establishing goals and ensuring that the corporate objective is being pursued in development of new directions.

business risk exclusion   A clause in a liability insurance policy stating that no protection is granted for losses resulting from misrepresentation of products. Damages resulting from misstatements concerning safety under certain conditions, for example, will not be reimbursed by the insurance carrier.

business trust   A specialized, temporary form of organization. Assets shared by partners in a venture are held in trust. The trustee is responsible for managing the business. Partners in the trust receive certificates of beneficial interest, which are comparable to shares of stock and serve as proof of ownership in the trust. The trust itself may operate as a corporation or as a partnership. This organization is also called a Massachusetts trust or common-law trust.

buy and sell agreement   An agreement entered into by partners or shareholders in a closely held corporation. The agreement sets forth the terms and conditions under which a disabled or deceased partner's or shareholder's equity will be transferred to the remaining individuals or to the company. Such an agreement may also be instituted for a sole proprietorship, in which an employee or a group of employees would have the right to buy the equity of a disabled or deceased owner.

buy-back agreement   A provision in a sale contract stating that, under certain conditions, the seller agrees to repurchase property at a stated price.

   Example: An employee purchases a home and is relocated by a new employer. Included in the contract is a buy-back provision. It states that, if the buyer does not remain in the area for less than six months, the seller will repurchase the home at a specified price.

buying incentive   An inducement to a customer to buy a product. Incentives may include contests, discounts, or bonus product offers.

bylaws   Rules of conduct for a corporation, adopted at the time of formation and amended as the board of directors may later determine. The bylaws define the rights and duties of stockholders, directors, and officers, and indicate limits on the power that each management level may exert through action and decision.

byte   Eight bits (binary digits). The size of a computer is described in terms of its ability to process and store bytes. *See* bit.

C

CAD, CADD   *See* computer-aided design.

computer-aided design (CAD)   (also known as *computer-aided design and drafting* (CADD)   A software program used by engineers and architects to create two- and three-dimensional graphic displays from a series of specifications. They can modify the plans as desired without duplicating the effort, and they do not need to create physical models during the development process.

cafeteria plan   A range of employee benefits available on a selective basis. Rather than imposing the same benefits on all employees, whether needed or not, each individual is allowed to select from the range. A limited dollar amount of benefit is available and, depending on each employee's status, a mix of different benefits is allowed.

> **Example:** One employee has a working spouse whose health insurance plan covers both. So she does not select health insurance, but places a larger dollar amount in retirement. Another employee does not have a working spouse but needs better health insurance coverage.

call book   A record maintained by a salesperson, listing the names and addresses and other useful information on customers, leads, visits, and sales efforts.

cancellation clause   A contractual clause spelling out conditions under which the agreement may be reversed or cancelled. For example, a lease might provide that the landlord may terminate the lease if the property is sold.

capital   The equity of a business, consisting originally of money invested; and later of the combined additional paid-in capital, less owners' draws (in a partnership) or dividends paid out (in a corporation); and retained earnings in a profit and loss account. The sum of all capital accounts is referred to as net worth (sole proprietorship or partnership) or shareholders' equity (corporation), and is equal to all assets less all liabilities of the company.

capital asset   An asset purchased and put into use that must be depreciated over a recovery period. In comparison, an expense is written off in the year purchased. The distinction often is made on the basis of cost expected, useful life of the asset, and the use and purpose. Capital assets are classified on the balance sheet as long-term (or fixed) assets. Their gross value is reduced by a reserve for depreciation. Each year's depreciation expense is recorded against the reserve until the asset's entire depreciable value has been used up. At that point, a depreciable asset will have a book value of zero. Land, however, is a capital asset that cannot be depreciated.

capitalization   The total funds available to carry and fund operations. Capitalization may consist of a mixture of equity capital (stockholders' or owner's/partners' equity); and debt capital (loans and notes).

capital structure   The combined capitalization of a company, including both debt and equity. Debt may consist of short- and long-term notes. Equity may include one or more classes of stock, capital surplus, additional paid-in capital, retained earnings, and treasury stock. A comparison of capital structure between similar companies and the changing proportions of debt and equity over time are indications of an organization's capital strength.

cash accounting   One of two methods for keeping books, the other being the accrual method. Under the cash accounting system, transactions are entered into the books only when money changes hands. This is a simple method for keeping records, but it is far from accurate.

   Example: A company is granted a large contract at the end of the month and begins work. Although the income is earned, it is not booked until actually received. The company might spend a considerable sum of money on current expenses but not pay its bills for several weeks. A cash-based financial statement does not include the significant spending level.

   Although accrual accounting is more accurate, it also demands more detailed records, just to record and later reverse accruals of income, costs, and expenses. *See* accounting method; accrual accounting.

cash disbursements journal   A journal summarizing all payments made during a period. In a properly controlled journal, all checks are listed in numerical order and accounted for, even if voided. The distribution columns will balance with the total column in all cases, and summarized totals will be posted from the disbursements journal to the general ledger.

cash equivalence   The net market value of an asset. Upon sale, the cash equivalence may vary from the gross market value and the book value. For example, real estate's value may be drastically understated in the books. The purchase value of several years before does not reflect today's higher value; and the effects of depreciation will have diminished net value even more. Alternatively, assets may be discounted for a fast sale, or subject to selling expenses and costs. Cash equivalence is the net amount after deducting those expenses.

cash flow   The availability and degree of cash in the company. Cash flow is not the same as profit or loss, for a number of reasons. Profits must be adjusted by non–cash-basis sales, depreciation, investment in fixed assets, the sale of fixed assets, and principal payments on outstanding debts. The cash flow is summarized on the statement of cash flows, which accompanies the balance sheet and the income statement in the standard package of financial statements. Cash flow is controlled within the budgeting process through development and tracking of a cash flow projection. Cash flow is essential for the continued health of operations. If working capital is not maintained at adequate levels, it will become increasingly difficult to fund current operations without obtaining outside debt capital. The resulting interest payments may further deteriorate working capital, making the cash flow problem worse.

cash flow projection   A summary of estimated cash flow in the future, and a form of cash flow budgeting. The projection attempts to anticipate the receipt and disbursement of cash that will occur during the coming year and to set standards for management of working capital. It includes adjustments for depreciation and other noncash expenses, payments of principal on outstanding notes, changes in inventory or accounts receivable, increases or decreases in liabilities, and planned timing of the purchase or sale of capital assets. The decision to commit funds to projects, acquisitions, or investments may be timed with cash flow problems and opportunities in mind.

cash flow statement (also known as *source and application of funds statement*)   One of three financial statements prepared for a company, the other two being the balance sheet and the income statement. The cash flow statement is a summary of all sources and applications of funds. Sources include income expressed on a cash basis (adjusted for accrued income, depreciation, and other noncash items); proceeds from the sale of assets; invested capital; and proceeds from loans and other debts. Applications include purchases of capital assets; payments on notes and other liabilities; and net operating losses expressed on a cash basis.

cash receipts journal (also known as *cash journal* or *sales journal*)   A journal summarizing all cash receipts for a month. Included are receipts of income for the current month, as well as money received on account and representing payments of accounts receivable from previous periods. When the cash receipts journal is also used to summarize all sales, it will also include a summary of all sales made on account.

casualty insurance   Insurance protection against losses resulting from unexpected or unpredictable occurrences, also known as acts of God; all forms of insurance coverage protecting against losses due to negligence or liability due to monetary assessment of the value of the loss.

catastrophic loss   An unpredictable loss that will create a significant financial loss or hardship. Insurance protecting against a catastrophic loss is essential to many businesses. The test is whether or not the company would be able to survive, given the economic hardship or loss that could result from the catastrophe. Even if there is only a slim chance it could occur, the event itself could spell disaster, making it impossible to not have insurance.

cathode-ray tube (CRT)   The monitor or computer screen used to view information during processing or in review.

centralization   A form of organization that discourages or forbids delegation of authority or sharing of responsibilities. For example, in a centralized environment, one department or committee takes charge of preparing budgets for all departments. In a decentralized environment, a central office coordinates the efforts of each department, but each is responsible for developing its budget independently.

centralized budget   A budget prepared in one department or committee, rather than in each department. The centralized system is efficient in the sense that the entire procedure is limited to one area. A drawback is that departmental and divisional decision makers are not given the involvement needed for truly effective budgeting in all cases. Budgets may be prepared on a hybrid system, in which the best features of centralized and decentralized budgeting are achieved.

central limit theorem   A rule of statistics stating that the average of a set of identically spaced outcomes or values will exhibit a normal distribution. This means that the curve of outcomes on a scale will be symmetrical.

central processing unit   The system unit of a computer that manages and decodes information and executes the operator's instructions.

central tendency   A summary of statistical data through one of three measurements: mean, median, or mode. The mean, or average, is the most popular method for establishing financial forecasting and monitoring tools. The median is the middle value in a distribution, when values are arranged in ascending or descending order. The mode is the value or values that appear more than once in a distribution. These processes summarize information to permit interpretation. For example, a report might include the average value or the typical or expected outcome. The use of central tendency is common in business, because raw data by itself is difficult to judge. In evaluating the success of a new division, management may want to compare sales and profits to the "normal" outcome for a first year, meaning some form of central tendency must be used. *See also* mean; median; mode.

certified financial statement   A financial statement that results from the thorough and independent examination of an outside auditor. The auditor attaches a certification saying that, in the auditor's opinion, the statement reflects conditions and/or operations fairly and completely, and that it was prepared in accordance with generally accepted auditing standards. However, if the auditor believes that the statement does not conform to these standards, then the certification will include a qualified opinion. In that instance, the reasons for qualification may be given specifically, or the entire statement may be qualified.

chain of command   The top-to-bottom hierarchy of an organization, in which authority levels are identified and distinguished. At the top are the stocholders (in a corporation) or owners (in a partnership or sole proprietorship). Beneath that are the top management layers, with descending management levels following. A clear identification of the chain of command is essential in order to ensure smooth operations.

characters per second (CPS)   The number of type characters per second a printer outputs from a computer. Knowledge of a printer's capability provides a basis for comparison with other printers, as well as a basis to estimate printing time of a document.

chart of accounts   A coded listing of all accounts in the general ledger. A logical numbering system assigns digits to identify the type of account. An example of coding logic includes giving first-digit value to distinct classifications of accounts:

Type of Account	Digit
Asset	1
Liability	2
Net worth	3
Sales	4
Direct costs	5
Expenses	6

The chart of accounts enables bookkeepers and accounting employees to prepare journals without having to contend with alphabetical titles. The chart of accounts is used for efficiency in developing and posting journals, even on a strictly manual basis. However, on an automated system, numerical coding saves time and effort and is essential.

chip   Part of a microprocessor, an electrical circuit developed in the transistor industry.

circle graph (also known as a *pie chart*)   A graphic in which a stationary outcome is reported. The circle graph is appropriate for a limited number of applications for breaking down 100 percent of an out-come. For example, a company may use the circle graph to report distribution of sales (100 percent) to direct costs, variable and fixed expenses, taxes, and profit; or it may show gross sales by division. The circle graph is not appropriate for reporting trends, since these are moving and developing over time.

The circle graph is developed by first devising the breakdown of 100 percent. Next, the 360 degrees of the circle are broken down along the same lines. For example, if direct costs represent 55 percent of sales, then 198 degrees of the circle have to be dedicated to direct costs:

$$55\% \times 360 \text{ degrees} = 198 \text{ degrees}$$

The entire circle is broken down in this manner. To construct the graph, divide the circle into degrees using a protractor. Draw a line from the exact middle of the circle to the outside rim; this becomes the base line. Place the protractor on the base line and locate the appropriate degree. Draw a line from the middle to the rim at that point; this line becomes the base line for the next calculation. Follow this procedure until the entire breakdown has been completed.

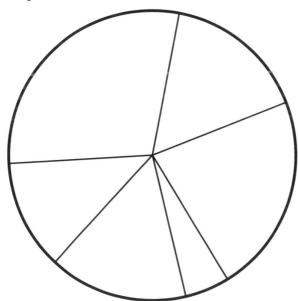

civil liability   Liability related to wrongs of other than a criminal nature. Included are negligence and omissions that lead to personal injury.

closely held corporation   A corporation whose voting stock is held or controlled by a few individuals. In such a company, the majority of voting stock may not be available for public trading, although some shares may be traded on public exchanges.

closing the books   The process undertaken by the bookkeeper at the end of the fiscal year. Each sales, direct cost, and expense account balance is reduced to zero, and the net of all those accounts is transferred to the "profit and loss" account in the equity section. At the beginning of the new year, all balances of asset, liability, and net worth accounts (which, upon closing, equal out to zero) are carried over to the new year.

   The books may be closed at the end of each month or quarter in order to prepare financial statements. The process is usually less formal than at year-end. For the purpose of interim statements, the balances are transferred to a worksheet and closing entries are made as pencil journals, not actually entered into the books.

cluster sample   In statistics, a random sample drawn from a larger sample which was previously put together in a nonrandom manner.

   Example: A company isolates 300 male purchasers between the ages of 35 and 40. This is a nonrandom sample. However, it later chooses a cluster sample of 50 men from the first group, on which a product preference test is performed.

COBOL   Acronym for Common Business-Oriented Language, a program language used for business programs.

code   Symbols representing information or instructions; a system used to abbreviate data such as name, or address, or one of several identifying numbers.

collection ratio   A financial ratio used to calculate the average number of days required to collect an outstanding account receivable. To calculate, divide the average accounts receivable balance by the average daily charge sales. The result is the number of days needed to collect. This ratio is useful in establishing and following trends. However, development of a fair average is a requirement in order to develop a reliable basis for analysis

$$\frac{A}{B} = D$$

A = Average receivables balance
C = Charge sales
D = Days needed to collect

collective bargaining   The process by which labor unions negotiate with management for a contract governing wages, hours, work rules, pension contributions, health benefits, and other issues affecting the hourly paid work force.

combination   A formula showing the number of different possible arrangements of outcome among several possible outcomes, when the order of occurrence is not interchangable.

>   **Example:** A manager must assign five people to a project team. There are eight people available. Since no one person may fill more than a single slot, the combination formula can be applied to determine how many possible outcomes there are. This distinguishes the combination from the permutation.

$$_nC_r = \frac{n!}{r!(n-r)!}$$

N = Number of factors
C = Combinations
r = Number of arrangements
! = Factorial

command-driven program   A program in which the user is required to enter commands to get desired results, rather than making a selection from an array of choices. *See* menu-driven program.

committee   A specialized group of individuals brought together to execute a short-term project, study a problem or range of problems, or arrive at a decision. The committee is usually authorized and formed by a decision-maker for a finite period and given a precise range of tasks. A committee is generally less effective than a more action-oriented project team or department given a similar assignment.

common stock   An equity security representing partial ownership of a corporation. Common stockholders are usually allowed to vote on issues concerning the overall direction and management of the company; however, the stockholder is not involved in day-to-day operations. Preferred stockholders enjoy a priority of payment in the event of liquidation, over both debtors and common stockholders. However, common stock yields the most in terms of income, in the form of dividends declared by the board of directors.

common stock ratio (also known as *capitalization test*)   A ratio showing the porportion of total capital represented by common stock. To compute, (1) add the total of common stock, capital surplus, and retained earnings; (2) divide the result by total capitalization (equity plus long-term bonds). Capitalization consists of the sum of equity positions plus debt capital.

$$\frac{C + S + E}{T} = R$$

C = Common stock T = Total capitalization
S = Capital surplus R = Common stock ratio
E = Retained earnings

comparative negligence   A theory under tort law stating that two or more defendants may share negligence in varying degrees. Unlike contributory negligence, in which someone bringing suit may share in the negligence to a degree, comparative negligence refers strictly to a sharing of responsibility among defendants. For example, a manufacturer fails to test for defects and a distributor makes false claims that the product was, in fact, tested. Both defendants might share in the negligence, with the degree of blame to be determined by the court. *See* contributory negligence.

comparative statement   A financial statement that shows results for both the current period and a past period or periods. In most situations, the past period is one identical to the current period. For example, a three-month current income statement would be compared to the same three months of the previous year.

When comparative statements are prepared, great care should be taken to ensure that all accounts are reflected on a like basis. For example, if certain payroll expenses are shown as expenses one year, but as direct costs in the following year, the comparative statement will not accurately show the change from one period to the next. A worksheet adjustment is required.

compensatory stock option   An option given to employees as part of their compensation. The value is measured by a formula. The quoted market price as of the date the option is given, minus the option price the employee is required to pay, equals the compensation level. The date on which this measurement takes place is the earliest date when both the number of shares to be issued and the issue price are revealed.

compilation   A form of financial statement that is not accompanied by an auditor's qualified opinion. It is an expedient form of financial statement that also saves time. The compilation may include a description of limited tests the auditor performed or may simply specify that the books and records were not subject to a detailed review.

completed contract accounting   An accounting method in which income, costs, expenses, and profit or loss are not booked until the job has been completed. Under this method, a substantial net profit may be deferred until a later period. It is far from accurate for the purpose of tracking information. However, it presents tax advantages to the company. Completed contract accounting is allowed only under restricted circumstances.

Example: A contracting firm is currently working on a job being tracked on the completed contract method. As of the end of the current year, the job is 92 percent complete. That includes a net profit of $485,000. However, none of the revenue or costs will be reflected on this year's books. It will all be recognized next year, when the job is 100 percent complete.

See also accounting method.

compound interest   Interest paid on interest over time, at a predetermined interval. Interest may be compounded daily, monthly, quarterly, semiannually, or annually. The more frequent the compounding, the higher the interest.

To calculate compound interest, first divide the stated, or nominal, annual rate by the number of compounding periods. For monthly compounding, there are 12 periods; for quarterly compounding, there are 4 periods. The result is the periodic rate. Multiply this rate by the principal amount. Each subsequent period's interest will be higher, because interest is being compounded.

A comparative example shows how compounding works. The chart below shows simple interest at 8 percent, next to quarterly compounding. The annual rate is divided by 4 (quarters), producing a periodic rate of 2 percent:

	Simple Interest			Compound Interest	
Quarter	*Interest*	*Total*	*Quarter*	*Interest*	*Total*
		100.00			100.00
1	2.00	102.00	1	2.00	102.00
2	2.00	104.00	2	2.04	104.04
3	2.00	106.00	3	2.08	106.12
4	2.00	108.00	4	2.12	108.24

See simple interest.

comprehensive insurance   Any form of insurance that provides coverage for two or more different forms of loss.

compromise leadership   Descriptive of a manager who attempts to use both a task and a relationship orientation, often in situations where only one of the two, or neither, is appropriate. This manager is perceived as unable to effectively make decisions and as one who responds poorly to pressure. *See also* task–style leadership.

concept test   A form of research in which consumer reaction is judged, not to a specific product, but to ideas for a new product or product line.

conditional contract   A contract that becomes enforceable only upon completion of a contingency or some future event. For example, a contract specifies that performance will occur (such as payment for property) if that property passes a contractor's inspection. If there are defects the seller is not willing to cure, no contract will exist.

conditional sale   **1.** An agreement to sell and to then repurchase under specified conditions, at a later date, or for a specified price. **2.** An agreement to transfer possession and the right of use in property, but to withhold title until a specified performance has occurred, usually full payment of the purchase price. Upon completion of the performance condition, the sale becomes absolute.

condition concurrent   A contractual provision stating that two separate events might happen at the same time. The provision usually relates to matters of performance.

condition precedent   A contractual provision stating that one event or action must occur before a subsequent, specified action can take place.

condition subsequent   A contractual provision specifying that an action or event may not take place until a preceding action or event has been completed.

conflict of interest   A condition in which an individual or company is in the position of having a direct interest in the outcome of a decision, while being responsible for protecting the rights of another party.

> **Example:** An arbitrator is asked to decide a dispute. However, the outcome could affect the value of land or stock the arbitrator owns. That presents a conflict of interest, since the arbitrator could not fairly decide the outcome.

consideration   Payment or other compensation given in exchange for equal consideration or for performance. Under contract law, consideration must be specified and equal on both sides in order for the contract to be legal and valid. A legal contract cannot exist if only one side is expected to provide consideration.

consignment selling   A form of merchandising in which the supplier's goods are placed in stores and made available to customers. However, payment for those goods is made only if and when they are sold. The merchant has the right to return any unsold goods, usually by a specified date.

consolidated statement   A financial statement showing results for all operations, subsidiaries, and divisions. In many companies, divisions act independently and do not review financial results on a consolidated basis except at year-end. The consolidated statement shows stockholders how combined operations resulted during the year, even though the divisions and subsidiaries may be very unrelated.

consolidation loan   A loan that combines other, previously written loans. The consolidation loan is convenient and it averages the interest rates of other loans. Because it is a form of refinancing, it differs somewhat from the wraparound loan. However, in many uses, the two terms are used to describe the same situation.

consumer profile   A marketing study that lists the demographic, psychological, or geographic attributes of customers who purchase a particular product. The profile is especially useful if it demonstrates how the attributes of the customer differ from those of the total population.

continuing discrimination   A condition in which identified past abuses of a discriminatory nature have not been corrected by an employer. The term implies knowledge of the problem on the part of the employer. However, knowledge is not required in order for the condition to exist. A case could be made that the continuing discrimination was a consequence of knowledge the employer should or could have acquired but did not.

continuous audit   A procedure practiced by internal auditing departments. Rather than waiting for the end of the period and then conducting a detailed audit in a very short period of time, the department investigates procedures throughout the year. The advantage of the continuous audit is that it spreads the auditor's work evenly throughout the year. In addition, it may lead to the discovery of control lapses or expensive procedures. The sooner those procedures are discovered and corrected, the more likely that losses will be cut or reduced.

contract   An agreement between two or more parties that some level of performance will occur, based on consideration exchanged. The contract must be legal in order to be binding; each party must be legally competent to enter into the agreement; and the agreement must exist to an extent that both sides agree to its terms, a concept in law called a meeting of the minds.

contributory negligence   A theory in tort law stating that negligence may be shared between the individual defendant and the individual suffering the loss.

Example: A company owns its own building and leases parts to other tenants. One tenant sues the company/landlord when equipment is damaged as the result of a water leak. The court determines, however, that the tenant *and* the landlord share in the negligence. While the landlord was responsible for maintaining the roof, the tenant failed to notify the landlord of the problem for several days.

Contributory negligence is distinguished from comparative negligence, which is a theory stating that two or more defendants may share in responsibility for negligence. *See* comparative negligence.

control base **1.** In statistics, an attribute of the entire sample under study that enables one to analyze and conclude. **2.** In market research, a region that is not tested but, it is assumed, can be measured in the same way as an area that was tested. Thus, any differences between test and control samples are meaningful in monitoring the outcome of a test.

controlled corporation A corporation whose voting stock is 51 percent or more owned or controlled by one person or organization, or by a group in unified agreement, but which does not directly manage the corporation. A subsidiary is an example of a controlled corporation. The parent company does not take part in day-to-day operations, but it does control the voting stock.

control system A system or idea put into effect in a company or department for the purpose of controlling spending or safeguarding assets. The system may be as simple as the requirements for reimbursement from a petty cash fund or as complex as methods for preventing theft of inventory. Control systems are designed to save money by protecting assets and cutting expensive and unnecessary procedures.

coping behavior Behavior practiced by individuals whose goals are blocked. Using the trial-and-error approach, the individual replaces a previous goal with one more likely to work. The result: The person's need to succeed is met.

Example: An employee has the personal goal of becoming the department manager. However, it becomes apparent that the job will be given to someone else. The employee accepts the position of supervisor, working under the newly appointed manager of the department. This is typical coping behavior.

corporate campaign   An advertising program aimed at improving or maintaining the corporate image rather than selling more product.

corporation   A legal entity that is owned by one or more stockholders. In the event an individual stockholder wants to sell shares, a new owner is located, but the organization continues. In comparison, when ownership in a sole proprietorship or partnership changes, the organization must be dissolved and a new one formed. The corporate stockholder has some protection from liability for actions of the corporation and its employees.

correspondent bank   A bank that performs banking services for another bank in an area not available to the second bank. This includes a depository relationship and facilitating of transactions between states.

   Example: A major bank in New York acts as correspondent for a major bank in California. The second bank performs the same service for the New York institution. The two may compensate one another based on the nature of the transactions between them; or they may assume that the value of each service is equal, and no compensation is required except in unusual cases.

cost accounting   The breakdown in detail of direct costs and, often, of expenses as well, into cost centers, jobs, or product lines. The purpose of the analysis and breakdown is to identify degrees of profitability. Cost accounting has valid applications in production and manufacturing environments, but is of limited value in service and retail organizations. *See* cost center.

cost allocation   The method used to assign direct costs to individual product lines. Costs may be divided on the basis of sales percentages, direct labor, square footage, or some other means. In a fair allocation system, the method is not arbitrary, and is justified. The key to this is identification of the logical means that defines costs as they are incurred. An arbitrary method is inherently inaccurate.

cost center   A department, division, or area to which costs are allocated; or, in a non–cost-accounting environment, a term often applied to a nonselling department, region, or division.

cost of goods sold   The total cost of materials, direct labor, and other direct costs, plus or minus any change in inventory for the period.

The cost of goods sold is the direct cost of generating sales. When it is subtracted from sales for the period, the result is gross profit.

cost of living allowance (also known as *cost of living adjustment,* or *COLA*)   An adjustment to wages and salaries to reflect the increased cost of living, usually as measured by change in the consumer price index. The percentage of increase in the index is applied to the earnings level.

cost per return   A method of determining the effectiveness of a promotion. A sales offer or contest is announced, inviting a direct response from the buyer. To determine cost per return, divide the total advertising cost by the number of responses.

cost per thousand   The amount of money required for advertising to reach one thousand customers.

cottage industry   Any industry in which the goods or services offered to the customer are generated from the company owner's home rather than in an outside factory or office. The term also refers to industries whose employees work at home with their own equipment, but who are not independent businesses. In the latter half of the twentieth century, cottage industries in the United States have expanded rapidly. Some experts predict that by the middle of the twenty-first century, cottage industries will, collectively, represent a larger portion of the business economy than larger, publicly traded companies.

covenant not to compete   An agreement to not enter a competing business within a specified area and for a specified period of time. This agreement occurs upon sale of a business or formation of a company involving transfer of rights.

CP/M   Control Program for Microprocessors, a standard operating system that is used on a wide range of different hardware.

CPS   *See* characters per second.

CPU   *See* central processing unit.

creative financing   Any type of financing other than that offered by a conventional or government lender, often involving unusual terms. Creative financing includes graduated payments, interest rate buy-downs, and interest-only payments with balloon payments due at the end of the term. The motives for creative financing usually are that borrowers cannot qualify for conventional financing due to their income or credit history.

credit   The right-hand side of an entry in the double-entry bookkeeping system. The sum of all credits should always equal to the sum of all debits. When the two sides are not equal, the books are not yet in balance.

cross training   A method of expanding job coverage while also helping employees to develop broader job skills. Each employee is trained to perform in two different jobs within the department. In the event of unexpected and extended leaves of absence or termination of any one employee, another is available to continue performing the tasks of the job. Although the theory is a sensible one, application is more difficult. Because jobs tend to evolve and change constantly, it is difficult for a cross-trained individual to keep pace with tasks that are not part of the daily routine.

CRT   *See* cathode-ray tube.

cumulative liability   **1.** The limit a company places on the total amount of risk of a specific type that it will insure against, including risks ceded to other companies. **2.** The limit an insurer will allow one insured individual or company to have for all types of liability insurance coverage.

current assets   All assets owned by a company that are in the form of cash or are convertible to cash within one year or less. Included are accounts receivable, current notes receivable, inventory, and any marketable securities. Current assets and liabilities are studied to judge working capital and the company's ability to pay for operating expenses out of currently available funds.

current liabilities   All debts of the company that are due and payable within one year or less. Included are accounts payable, accrued liabilities and taxes, and 12 months' worth of payments on outstanding notes. The net difference between current assets and current liabilities is called working capital. A study of trends in working capital indicates how well management controls cash flow.

current ratio   A financial ratio comparing current assets (cash and assets convertible to cash within 12 months) to current liabilities (liabilities payable within the next 12 months). To calculate, divide current assets by current liabilities. Any current ratio below 2 to 1 is considered a sign of lower than acceptable management of working capital. The current ratio should be reviewed as the latest entry in a long-term trend. Unlike many other ratios, however, the expected 2 to 1 or better standard may be broadly applied to a number of companies.

$$\frac{A}{L} = R$$

A = Current assets
L = Current liabilities
R = Current ratio

current value accounting   A form of accounting that attempts to reflect values in current terms, rather than under less realistic and more conservative guidelines. For example, generally accepted accounting standards dictate that capital assets are to be carried at cost value less depreciation. However, some capital assets, such as real estate, tend to increase in value. Under the current value accounting system, the real estate would be carried at an estimated or appraised current value, properly reflecting the conditions and current values of business assets, liabilities, and operations. If the asset's value is increased, it must also be assumed that a paper profit would be reflected during the period of increase.

current yield   The yield being paid on a bond at the current value of the bond. When a bond is valued at par (100), the current yield is the same as the nominal yield. However, when the bond is valued at a premium or at a discount, the current yield changes. As the bond's value is discounted, current yield rises; as the value takes on a premium, current yield falls.

   Example: A $1,000 bond yielding 8 percent ($80 per year) is discounted to 96 on today's market. So it has a market value of $960. The current yield is:

$$\frac{\$80}{\$960} = 8.33\%$$

   Example: A $1,000 bond yielding 8 percent ($80 per year) currently is selling at a premium of 104. A $1,000 bond is worth $1,040. The current yield is:

$$\frac{\$80}{\$1040} = 7.69\%$$

$$\frac{I}{M} = Y$$

I = Annual interest
M = Market price
Y = Current yield

cursor   **1.** A point, symbol, or blinking light on a computer screen, showing the operator the location at which data will next be entered. **2.** The plotting pen in a CAD system.

custom software   A program or series of programs written specifically for one user. Custom software has special features requested by the user or required for a particular circumstance. In comparison, packaged software, which is purchased off the shelf, is identical for all users and contains no specialized features.

D

daily compounding One of the two methods of calculating compound interest each day. One is on a calendar basis, using a 365-day year. The other assumes twelve months, each with thirty days, for a total of 360 days per year.

To calculate, divide the annual rate by the number of days in the year. The sum is the daily interest rate. This rate is applied each day to the previous day's balance.

Example: Using the 360-day method, and assuming a nominal rate of 8 percent, the daily rate is:

$$\frac{0.08}{360} = 0.000222$$

Each day's balance is multiplied by this daily rate, so a deposit of $1,000 will earn 22 cents the first day:

$$\$1,000 \times 0.000222 = 0.22$$

On the second day, the new balance, $1,000.22 is multiplied by the daily rate. This procedure is continued each day for as long as the funds are left on deposit.

daisy wheel A circular print head used on a printer or typewriter. The wheel spins rapidly to the correct point, where a hammer strikes the letter against a ribbon. With faster, more reliable technology derived from dot matrix and laser jet printing, the daisy wheel is becoming obsolete.

data   In the context of computers, information input, stored, or processed within a computer system. In modern usage, *data* has taken on an expanded meaning to include all information, files, documents, or intelligence.

database   Interrelated records residing within a computerized system. Records in a *relational* database are linked together by way of programs, key fields, or storage location. Database files are cross-referenced, avoiding duplication and error and making processing much more efficient.

database management system (DBMS)   A form of software designed for storage of information in such a way that there is little or no duplication. Several different programs access the same database and use it for various functions, increasing efficiency. In comparison, a file management system relies upon the creation of files for each program or routine, with little or no cross reference from the database for different programs. Database management systems are far more useful and practical.

date of record (also known as *record date*)   The date identified for the purpose of paying dividends. Shareholders owning stock on that date are entitled to the payment. The dividend may be declared for payment to owners of stock as of a record date in the future, but with the actual payment to be made at yet another date. To avoid confusion, the date of record is the critical date for the identification of who is to receive dividends. *See* ex-dividend.

dba   *See* doing business as.

DBMS   *See* database management system.

debit   The left-hand side of an equal entry in the double-entry bookkeeping system. All debits and credits are equal in value to one another at all times, so that the balances of both sides will equal zero. When this condition is not present, the books are not in balance.

debt capital   Funds to carry on a business raised from bonds and long-term contracts payable. Stock, in comparison, is equity capital. The combination of debt and equity capital represent the total capitalization of a company.

Investors who assume a debt position are compensated in the form of interest, whereas equity investors receive dividends and may profit from increased market value of the stock. Equity investors also risk losing market value, but debt investors' positions are protected by a contractual promisory note. Debt investors usually also enjoy a priority of claims over equity investors.

debt coverage ratio   A financial ratio comparing net operating income to total loan payments made during the same year. This ratio tracks the ability of income to keep pace with and to fund the cost of acquiring debt capital. To calculate, divide net operating income by annual loan payments. The answer is expressed as the number of times, or coverages.

$$\frac{N}{P} = D$$

N = Net operating income
P = Annual loan payments
D = Debt coverage ratio

debt instrument   A written document or investment based on an outstanding debt: a promissory note, bond, or contract.

debt service   The combined interest and principal payment required during a period, most often one year, to pay a loan or bond. The principal portion may be in the form of payments or sinking fund allowances. Debt service may be level or scaled. In level debt service, the payment remains the same each month, but the amount going to principal gradually increases over the repayment period. This is the common schedule of repayment in fully amortized loans. A scaled repayment may be contracted as part of a variation in schedule (as in a graduated payment mortgage), or it may be the consequence of changing indexes as part of an adjustable rate mortgage. The contract limits the annual increases as well as the maximum increase over the life of the contract. If actual interest rates exceed those levels, the payments will be scaled to the maximum level each period. *See* sinking fund.

debt-to-equity ratio   A financial ratio comparing liabilities to tangible net worth. The ratio shows the trend over a period of time of the stable, increasing, or decreasing proportion between the equity and debt capitalization of the company. For example, if the debt portion increases, then a growing level of interest and debt service will be required, meaning less net income for shareholders in the future. To compute the debt-to-equity ratio, divide liabilities by tangible net worth. The result is expressed as a percentage.

$$\frac{L}{N} = D$$

L = Liabilities
N = Tangible net worth
D = Debt-to-equity ratio

decentralization   Descriptive of an environment in which authority and decision making occur at a number of locations. Delegation is emphasized and tests are devised to judge performance and results. In comparison, a centralized organization is one that does not test results but closely monitors and controls all aspects of operations from one location.

Example: In one company, the budgeting process is achieved in a decentralized manner. Each department prepares its own budget and submits it for approval to a budget review committee. The departments are expected to conform to a format for presenting and documenting the budget. Upon acceptance of each final budget, the companywide budget is prepared by the accounting department. Monthly review occurs on a companywide basis, but each department is called upon to explain significant individual variances.

decentralized budget   A budgeting system in which each department or division is entirely responsible for preparing and monitoring its own budget. While this is less efficient than centralized budgeting, it places control over the process within each profit or cost center. The major advantage of decentralized budgeting is that control is placed at the departmental or divisional level, where it can be exercised. The major disadvantage is that the company's management must exert greater effort to achieve uniform monitoring control over the entire budget.

decision tree   A diagram used to study and explain as many possible consequences or outcomes of a decision, or to test likely outcomes

at various phases of a decision-making process. This is used in
project management, in automation and programming, and in
analysis, to arrive at the most likely course of events, and to aid
decision making.

declining balance   A form of depreciation in which the amount
written off each year declines. The annual deduction is subtracted
from the asset's value each year, and the remainder subjected to the
same ratio of allowable depreciation.

   Example: An asset worth $8,000 has a 10-year recovery pe-
riod. The depreciation schedule calls for 200 percent declining
depreciation during the first four years, and reversion to straight-
line depreciation for the remaining six years. To compute the first
year (assuming a full year's depreciation is available), (1) compute
the straight-line depreciation:

$$\frac{\$8,000}{10} = \$800$$

(2) Multiply the straight-line rate by the declining balance rate, in
this case, 200 percent:

$$\$800 \times 200\% = \$1,600$$

   This allowable depreciation is deducted from the basis of the
asset, in order to compute depreciation for the following year. This
procedure is continued through the fourth year. The then-remaining
balance is depreciated at a straight-line rate for the remainder of the
10-year term. To arrive at the new straight-line rate, divide the
fourth year balance by the remaining six years.

$$\frac{\$3,277}{6} = \$546.16$$

Year	Depreciation	Balance
		$8,000
1	$1,600	6,400
2	1,280	5,120
3	1,024	4,096
4	819	3,277
5	547	2,730
6	546	2,184
7	546	1,638
8	546	1,092
9	546	546
10	546	0

deferred compensation plan   A retirement plan with terms stating that the employee is allowed to elect to not receive a portion of current earnings. The employer will invest the deferred compensation under guidelines of the plan, so that both compensation and income taxes are deferred into the future. The decision to defer income is irrevocable in order to qualify for Internal Revenue Service guidelines.

deferred contribution plan   An agreement under the terms of a profit sharing plan stating that an unused credit carryover from a previous year can be added to the employer's contribution in future years and become tax deductible for the employer.

deferred expense   An expense that will not be recognized until a future period. It remains on the books as an asset until the appropriate period.

> **Example:** A company purchases supplies in bulk, planning to use them the following month. However, the fiscal year ends. Appropriate treatment under the accrual accounting system is to defer the expense until the period in which the supplies are used.

deferred income   Income which, although received in the current period, is deferred until a later period, usually dictated by the appropriating accounting method in use. This is a correct decision when income is prepaid by a customer but will not be earned until a future period. The amount of deferred income is carried on the books as a liability until the time it will be reversed and recognized.

Example: A contractor is reporting income under the percentage-of-completion method. Through the end of the current month, the job is 65 percent complete; however, the contractor has received 70 percent of the income. According to the percentage of completion rules, five percent of the income should be deferred until it has been earned.

defined benefit plan   A pension plan under which future payments will occur at specified levels for each participating employee. Each employee is required, however, to work for a certain number of years. In some defined benefit plans, all contributions are made by the employer; in others, employees also contribute a portion of the accumulating fund. Any portion contributed by the employee is immediately 100 percent vested. For the part contributed by the employer, vesting occurs on a schedule allowed by current law.

defined contribution plan   A pension plan under which the employer agrees to contribute a specified amount each year, based on a formula. The formula may involve years of service, level of compensation, or age of the employee. The contribution level does not vary from the formula. However, there is no minimum guarantee of future benefits to be paid under the plan.

delegation   The sharing of authority and responsibility with others. Supervisors and managers may delegate to subordinates, just as top management may delegate on a broader scale to entire divisions, subsidiaries, or departments. Delegation frees up management's time to analyze and plan, without having to be concerned with more detailed concerns. Ideally, the higher one is on the corporate organization chart, the less detail should be involved in the day.

demand loan (also known as a *callable loan*)   A loan without a fixed due date. Principal is to be repaid at the lender's discretion. Such loans often allow for periodic adjustments or recalculations of interest. The borrower makes periodic payments of interest and principal or, in some instances, interest only.

democratic leadership   Descriptive of a management style in which employees are encouraged to participate directly in goal setting, planning, and determining actions of the team or department. In the best of circumstances, employees enjoy the freedom to participate and to affect outcome. In the worst of circumstances, the leader is not respected because a strong, decisive stand has not been taken.

The democratic leadership may be unable or unwilling to act decisively when circumstances demand a less democratic approach.

depletion A noncash expense of natural resources similar to depreciation. However, depreciation is applied to purchased capital assets. Depletion may be applied to timber, mineral and oil reserves, and other resources.

deposit administration plan A funding instrument for a pension plan. Premiums are deposited without allocation to specific benefit purchases in behalf of participating employees. Upon retirement, an annuity is purchased, with monthly income varying depending on the investment activities of pooled funds on deposit over a period of years. In some cases, the insurance company managing the deposit administration plan will guarantee a minimum interest percentage, either for a period of years or for the entire time the plan is active. The minimum guarantee will be exceeded if investment activity was better than expected. If investment activity was not as good as expected, however, the insurer is still required to honor its guarantee.

deposits in transit Deposits delivered to the bank and entered on the books and records, but not acknowledged by the bank as of their statement cutoff date. This creates a timing difference for purposes of reconciling the bank account. Deposits in transit are added to the reported balance on the bank statement in order to reconcile that balance to the balance shown on the company's books.

   Example: On the last business day of the month, a deposit of $4,000 was made. However, the bank had already cut off its month-end and mailed out statements. On the bank reconciliation, this is shown as a timing difference. It will appear as the first deposit in the following month, according to the bank.

depreciation A noncash expense made by way of a journal entry. Depreciation is a write-off of capital assets over a recovery period mandated by tax regulation. Companies may elect to claim depreciation under the prescribed method or one of several extended methods. A limited amount of annual capital expenditure may also be expensed, or written off, in the year the asset is placed into service.

   The entry to record depreciation is made by way of the journal, since no cash changes hands. A debit is made to depreciation expense, offset by a credit to the reserve for depreciation (or accumulated depreciation), which is a negative asset account. The gross value of the asset, minus the reserve total, equals the net book value of fixed assets. *See* accumulated depreciation.

descriptive statistics   Methods applied to study and summarize a series of numbers. These procedures are used frequently in a number of business applications. One of the best-known forms of descriptive statistics is calculation of mean, or average, used in budgeting and forecasting and other types of reports. Any method of summarizing information includes descriptive statistical techniques, such as expressing a trend in the form of a ratio rather than by presenting a long list of values. Attempting to communicate financial information without the use of descriptive methods would be difficult, if not impossible.

dilution   A theoretical value equaling the effect on earnings per common share of stock if all convertible securities were to be converted and warrants or options were to be exercised by their owners. The earnings per share would decline because a larger number of shareholders would participate in the available dividend pool.

direct cost   Spending that is directly related to sales and, accordingly, will rise and fall as sales rise and fall. Direct costs include materials purchased, increases and decreases in inventory levels, direct labor, freight, and other costs. When direct costs are deducted from sales, the result is gross profit. *See* cost of goods sold.

direct labor   Labor costs that vary in direct relationship to sales levels. The distinction between direct labor and salaries and wages (an expense) is the direct relationship of labor to sales. An expense will be incurred regardless of sales levels. Direct labor will increase during periods of higher sales, and will decrease when the opposite occurs. For example, a company pays manufacturing employees on an hourly rate. When work slacks off, workers are laid off and direct labor decreases. Administrative salaries are paid, however, regardless of volume levels. Administrative salaries are not direct costs, but are part of overhead.

direct mail advertising   Advertising achieved through the postal system to a targeted audience based on various demographic data such as household income, buying patterns, or location. Direct mail includes flyers, letters, and promotions aimed at getting customer response. It often involves incentives to act immediately, such as reduced rates or contests.

direct marketing Any form of marketing in which the promotional effort is made directly to the customer. This includes personal contact, giveaways, brochures, and other one-to-one contacts. Direct marketing is considered more effective than indirect methods, because it enables one person to speak directly with another.

direct overhead The part of fixed overhead allocated to the cost of manufacturing, calculated on a set schedule known as the burden rate. The process is the only consistent method for allocating overhead to the cost of goods sold, and involves detailed analysis of accounts to identify square footage usage and other means for making the allocation.

direct sales Sales made directly to the customer and not through a distribution system or agent. The expression is widely used in the magazine industry. Subscriptions are sold directly by the publisher through space advertising in the magazine or in other publications, for example, and not through a subscription agency.

disability buy-out Insurance issued to partners and corporations. In case of disability of a partner or key executive, the disability benefits will fund a buy-out of the disabled partner's or shareholder's interests. This is essential when two or more partners or shareholders in a small corporation would not be able to afford a buy-out from current assets. Without the insurance, in the event of the disability of a partner or shareholder, the remaining individuals would suffer an economic loss.

disbursements journal *See* cash disbursements journal.

disc *See* disk.

discounted cash flow A method for calculating the present value of future receipts or expenditures. It involves figuring a compound interest value based on the time involved between today and the expected time of receipt or payment. The discounted method is assumed to be more accurate than a straight calculation, because time value of money is included in the calculation. However, this assumes that a reasonable interest rate is applied to the calculation. To be reasonable, the rate must be based on a logical assumption. For example, one may calculate future profits using discounted cash flow, using the percentage equal to percentage of profit realized in the average year.

To calculate the discount, multiply the amount of money by a factor in a present value interest table. The reduced amount reflects today's present value, assuming that the money accumulates to 100 percent by the date in the future on which it will be received or paid. *See also* internal rate of return.

discrimination **1.** The illegal, selective, and unfair treatment of an individual on the basis of race, color, national origin, religion, sex, marital status, disability, or veteran status. **2.** The continuing failure to remedy past discrimination.

disk (also alternatively spelled *disc*) A magnetic storage device. The disk may be a floppy, or removable one of limited size, or a hard disk placed in or near the central processing unit and considered as a permanent storage area.

disk drive A device for reading, managing, and organizing a disk. It transmits information to the disk and back to working memory in response to commands.

disk operating system (DOS) A proprietary operating system from Microsoft Corporation stored on disk and used widely in micro-computers.

dispersion (spread) The degree of difference between values in a distribution and the average. It is the *degree* of dispersion that indicates the dependability of estimates. For example, compare the range of dispersion in these two columns:

Small Dispersion	Large Dispersion
27	4
31	18
32	57
34	106
36	192

The narrow dispersion in the first column means that each value is relatively close to the average value of the entire column. As the second column's values have a much wider dispersion, any estimates based on these raw data will be far less dependable.

distribution A list of numbers, or raw data. The distribution forms the basis for statistical analysis. For example, to calculate mean, or average, you must first identify a list of values (the distribution). You then add up the items in the list and divide them by the number of values in the distribution.

dividend A distribution of a company's net earnings to stockholders in a corporation, usually made quarterly. The board of directors determines the amount, which is not necessarily the entire profit available. For example, the board may reinvest part or all of the profits to fund expansion and future market value of the stock.

Dividends are usually paid in cash. However, the board of directors may declare a stock dividend, in which case current stockholders are given additional shares with market value. They may convert those shares to cash by selling them on the open market.

Example: A corporation declares a 10 percent stock dividend for stockholders of record as of March 10. All stockholders having stock as of that date will receive an additional share for every ten shares owned.

dividend payout ratio A financial ratio that allows for the analysis of a dividend's value, without being distorted by ever-changing market value of the stock. To compute, divide dividends on common stock by the net income less any dividends paid on preferred stock. The result is expressed as a percentage.

$$\frac{D}{N-P} = R$$

D = Dividends on common stock
N = Net income
P = Dividends on preferred stock
R = Dividend payout ratio

documentation Written instructions that explain a computerized (or other) system. Documentation may be used to train, to locate and correct bugs, or to aid in programming itself. It describes the logic of the system, often using graphics, breaks down routines into connected steps and identifies decision points in processing.

doing business as (DBA)   A designation used for companies using a fictitious business name. For example, a company (corporation, partnership, or sole proprietorship) called ABC Company is conducting business under the name XYZ Company. The correct description of this is ABC Company, dba XYZ Company.

dollar volume discount   A discount allowed to a customer as an incentive to purchase a higher than average amount of merchandise, measured in dollars spent rather than in the number of items purchased.

domestic corporation   A corporation operating in the state in which it was incorporated. In other states, the same corporation is referred to as a foreign corporation.

domicile   The permanent place of residence of an individual or operation of a business.

dominant leadership   The most common form of leadership, characterized by establishment of a clear line of authority. The dominant leader may be able to delegate, allow and encourage participation in varying degrees, and strike a balance between task and human orientation, to a greater degree than leaders with a more specific focus to their style.

DOS   *See* disk operating system.

dot matrix   A format of printing in which each character is created from a field of dots rather than in fixed, solid form. Dot matrix is faster than fixed character alternatives, but quality varies based on the space between dots in the field. In higher-quality printers, output is indistinguishable from letter-quality printing in all ways except the shape of certain characters, but some speed is sacrificed.

double-declining balance (DDB)   A form of accelerated depreciation in which the calculated straight-line rate is doubled; also called 200 percent depreciation. This form of depreciation is called declining because the write-off falls each year, as does the depreciable base of the asset.

> **Example:** An asset with a basis of $7,000 can be depreciated over 10 years using the 200 percent declining balance method.

(1) Divide the asset value by the period involved to arrive at the straight-line depreciation:

$$\frac{\$7,000}{10} = \$700$$

(2) Multiply the straight-line amount by the applicable percentage for declining balance:

$$\$700 \times 200\% = \$1,400$$

This is the first year's allowed depreciation. It will decline in subsequent years, since depreciation already claimed is deducted from the basis. The basis in the second year will be $5,600 ($7,000 less $1,400). The decline will continue until the final year, when all remaining value can be written off as depreciation.

double-entry system   The most commonly used system of bookkeeping. Each entry in the books is assigned two equal sides, a debit (left) and a credit (right). These are not plus and minus designations, only left and right sides of the system. The purpose is to (a) ensure that the books are correctly posted and balanced, and (b) provide a complete record of each transaction. For example, when a cash-basis sale is completed, two accounts are affected. Cash is increased, and so is the balance of sales. The two-sided entry achieves both sides of the required entry. If the sale was earned but not yet paid, the entry would be to debit accounts receivable and credit sales. In a later period, when the payment is received, cash is debited and accounts receivable is credited. *See* single-entry system.

E

earnings per share (EPS)   The amount of average profit per share of common stock, computed as a means for tracking share value over time. The comparison is often seen in annual reports, showing growth in EPS from one year to the next. It is not a dormant statistic, but an ever-changing one. It is usually reported quarterly, and reflects all positive and negative activity of the company.

   Example: A company with 20 million shares that earned $40 million last year has current EPS of $2. If the company had to set aside a $10 million reserve for environmental cleanup, EPS would be $1.50.

economic life   The number of years a capital asset is expected to remain in use. After the economic life has expired, the asset is assumed to be obsolete or worthless. The concept is used in accounting to determine fair and reasonable depreciable periods, and in insurance to calculate allowable claim losses.

   Economic life may also refer to the practical and affordable life of machinery. For example, when annual maintenance expenses exceed a predetermined level, it may make more sense to trade in the machinery. At that point, the machinery has reached the end of its economic life.

economic value   The current market value of property which, for insurance purposes, is often the same as replacement cost value, net of depreciation.

edit   1. The validation of data placed in a computer system. The edit may be performed on a bath of information isolated by day or by part-day, to ensure that a larger body of information does not contain errors.

2. The process of checking text for grammatical and spelling errors, or to revise for clarity, before the final printout or publication.

electronic spreadsheet A program allowing the user to store and process numerical data in a large field of columns and rows. The boxes representing a matrix of a column and a row may be manipulated mathematically, providing sums, products, percentages, and so on.

eligible employee An employee who meets the qualifications for participation in a company-sponsored retirement plan, based on meeting the criteria as set forth in the plan. Typically an employee must work more than 20 hours per week; attain a specified number of service hours; be above the age of 21; and complete a specified number of months on the job before participation may begin.

embezzlement The misappropriation of cash or other assets, usually from an employer. Embezzlement may include crimes as small as theft of petty cash or as large as millions of dollars removed from company bank accounts. Many methods may be used, including some very elaborate systems for concealment. It is often detected only by a thorough audit of the books and records.

employee handbook A book listing the company's rules and policies regarding employment matters. This includes rules of attendance, dress, review and evaluation, and job performance, as well as observation of holidays, vacation policies, and benefits offered to employees. The handbook is considered under law as part of the contract between the employer and the employee. Thus, statements made in the handbook could be judged as discriminatory or as an implied promise or agreement that has been violated upon termination of employment. The handbook should be reviewed and audited with these points in mind.

employee stock option plan (ESOP) A program or benefit allowing employees to buy stock in the company. Once a certain level of ownership has been achieved, the ESOP, through trustees, participates in management of the organization. Ultimately, the employees, through the ESOP, control and then own the entire corporation. In addition to partial or full ownership, ESOPs may use dividends to pay down loans taken to buy stock.

endorsement   A provision added to an existing insurance policy to increase or add restrictions to the level of coverage.

entity plan   A buy-out agreement that allows an individual partner or stockholder (or a group) to purchase the interests of a disabled partner or stockholder. The buy-out benefit funds the purchase of partnership interests or corporate shares. *See also* disability buy-out.

EPS   *See* earnings per share.

equity capital   Usually a combination of stock, retained earnings, and additional paid-in capital; or, in the case of an unincorporated business, the owner's net equity. In comparison, debt capitalization includes notes and contracts payable and long-term bonds. Equity capital earns profits for investors and debt capital earns interest.

ESOP   *See* employee stock option plan.

excess contribution   An amount paid in to a qualified plan that is greater than the allowed annual contribution. The excess amount is subject to a penalty or an excise tax.

exclusions   The specified grouping of losses not covered by an insurance policy. The policy can (a) list exclusions specifically, or (b) indicate losses covered by the policy, with the provision that all other losses are excluded. For example, a business liability policy states that specific, named exclusions apply for certain activities, based on the type of company, activities engaged in during a manufacturing process, or risks associated with the type of product manufactured.

exclusive contract   A contract granted to one individual or business. The exclusive provision may last for only a limited period of time.

   Example: A company wishing to sell its home office building enters an exclusive contract with a real estate company for 90 days. After that period, the company may list the building with other brokerage firms if the exclusive company has not located a buyer.

ex-dividend   Status of stock when the record date has passed. This usually occurs about three weeks prior to actual payment of the dividend. The dividend is declared as being earned by shareholders of record as of the record date. The period between that date and the actual payment of the dividend is the ex-dividend period. *See* date of record.

executive committee   A high-level committee with members from top management. Its primary function is to agree upon and execute the actions dictated by the board of directors. The committee may also serve as an oversight group, reviewing financial reports and forecasts and approving financial decisions.

expectation value   An average that has been developed from observation of a number of random variable events. For example, the average salesperson in your company generates a specific level of sales per quarter, from which you may develop a standard for sales performance. Since the average has been rising over the past three years, you need to expand the observation by adding a factor for expectation value, reflecting the trend. To calculate, estimate the rate of increase and then apply assumptions about how it might continue. Weighted average techniques may also be used. *See* weighted average.

expense budget   A budget specifically for general and variable expenses, perhaps for a department, which excludes cash flow projections, direct cost estimates, or sales forecasts.

expenses   **1.** A category of the income statement for variable and fixed expenses. **2.** The grouping of expenditures below the gross profit line. **3.** The classification of expenses between gross profit and net profit. An expense applies to the current period only whereas a capital asset is depreciated over a number of years.

experience modification   An adjustment in premium on business insurance policies, based on actual losses experienced during a prior period. The adjustment may be an increase due to greater than expected losses or a decrease due to lower than expected or average losses.

exponential moving average   An efficient method of computing a weighted moving average. This method is especially efficient when working with a large field of values, or when computing the moving average frequently.

Example: If the field involves one value per month for an entire year, there will be 12 values. Determine the exponent by dividing 2 by the number of values in the field. The exponent in this case is:

$$\frac{2}{12} = 0.1667$$

Once the exponent has been computed, follow the steps in figuring the average. Each step can then be fit into a worksheet:

1. Figure the simple moving average for the first period.
2. Enter the value for the next period in the study.
3. Subtract the average in Step 1 from the value in Step 2.
4. Multiply the answer in Step 3 by the exponent.
5. Add the answer in Step 4 to the previous moving average. (If Step 4 is negative, subtract it.)

Period	Value	Prior Value	Result	Exponent	New Value	EMA

See average; moving average; weighted average.

external audit   An audit conducted by outside accountants or auditors rather than by employees of the company. An independent accountant's opinion may be necessary for certain types of financial reports.

extra dividend   A dividend declared over and above the normal and scheduled dividend.

Example: A corporation has been paying 25 cents per share every quarter for the past five years. This year, profits were exceptionally high, so the board of directors declared an extra dividend equal to 10 cents per share, after paying the usual 25 cents.

extraordinary item   Any nonrecurring adjustment or transaction included on a financial statement. Extraordinary items are usually footnoted and explained as separate items. For the purpose of year-to-year analysis, such items are removed before making a compari-son. For example, a company reports a nonoperating loss due to currency exchange fluctuations, affecting its overseas operations. Or, the valuation method for counting inventory is changed, creat-ing a one-time increase in net profits.

F

factoring **1.** A procedure used to raise capital using accounts receivable as collateral. The company sells its receivables to a factoring company, which pays a discounted value to the company and then collects the receivables. Receivables may be sold with or without recourse (with recourse, the company may repurchase them in the future). **2.** Gap financing for inventory during high-volume periods, in which case the factoring company may be a lender or finance company. In this instance, inventory serves as collateral for the temporary loan.

favorable variance A financial result in favor of the company, representing higher than expected sales or lower than expected costs or expenses. In terms of control and accuracy of estimates, the favorable variance may be viewed as being as much of a budgeting problem as an unfavorable variance.

   Example: Through the first six months, sales were forecast at $485 million. Actual sales were $550 million. Although this is favorable, it also may be indication of a serious oversight in the forecasting method. An analysis is undertaken to determine why the forecast was so far from actual results and improve the procedure for the following year.

feasibility study An analysis of factors involved in a proposed idea. The idea may be a project, a shift in markets or products offered, or an approach to a new market. The study identifies the variables and risk factors and compares those to the likely reward and costs involved. It then concludes that the idea is or is not feasible.

fidelity bond A form of insurance protecting against theft, embezzlement, and other dishonest acts of employees. The bond may be a blanket bond (applying to all employees) or coverage can be provided on a name-by-name basis.

field   **1.** In automation, a grouping of characters that are in some way related, representing a component of a record. Each record contains a specified number of fields (as in a database). **2.** In statistics, a number of values that will be treated in some manner (averaged, for example); a set.

FIFO   *See* first-in, first-out.

file   Information stored together in a series of records, representing the body of data on a particular topic or of a specific nature.

file management system   A series of programs, each containing its own data base. Programs access and manage data separately. In comparison, a database management system contains a single database and a number of different programs can access and manage the data.

    Example: A company using a file management system has a number of automated routines, all using customer information. Files duplicate certain types of information, including name and address. Thus, a lot of file space is taken up with duplicated information. In addition, when information changes, each file must be upgraded to reflect the change. When the company upgrades to a database system, the file management problem is resolved. All files are merged into a single database.

finance committee   A group of executives and managers, usually including financial and accounting leaders. The committee may be appointed by the board of directors, the chief executive officers, or the president of the company.

first-in, first-out (FIFO)   A method of valuing inventory, based on the assumption that the first items purchased were also the first items sold. Thus, any price changes subsequent to the purchase date affect items purchased for inventory later. The oldest prices are thus charged to the cost of goods sold. This method inflates profits during times of inflation, when inventory profits are created due to price changes. The last-in, first-out method is more widely used, since income taxes are reduced when inventory profits are eliminated. The charges to direct costs reflect current prices at all times. *See* last-in, first-out.

fiscal year (FY)   The 12-month period recognized by a company for tax purposes. The fiscal year for a corporation may begin and end in any month, with the only restriction being on frequency of change. A fiscal year may be selected to reflect the natural business year, which can vary from one industry to another.

five percent rule   A clause of co-insurance found in many property and casualty insurance policies. It states that when losses are lower than a minimum amount, or when thoses losses are lower than five percent of total value, an inventory or appraisal of the remaining property is not required.

fixed assets (also called *long-term assets*)   The capital assets of a business, subject to depreciation, depletion, or amortization; or nondepreciable assets, such as land. Capital assets are reduced by accumulated depreciation, representing annual write-offs booked according to a depreciation schedule.

fixed expenses   Overhead; expenses that do not change based on intermediate or small changes in sales volume. The fixed expense of an operation change as the result of expansion, downsizing, or new labor contracts.

   Example: Due to rapid expansion, the company hires many more clerical and home office employees. This creates the need for more office space, so upon expiration of the current lease, the company moves to larger and more expensive quarters. In this instance, "fixed" salaries and "fixed" rent expense both increased as the result of expansion. They will remain stable at this level, however.

flexible benefits   Benefits available to employees under a cafeteria plan. Employees are allowed a dollar level of total benefits, but are also allowed to select from an array of different benefits. For example, an employee whose spouse also works may elect to include no health benefit in his or her package. Another may want additional coverage combining health and major medical coverage.

flexible budget   A budget that calculates costs, expenses, and profits based on varying levels of sales volume. If sales increase rapidly, the expense level may be vastly different, which will then be reflected in net profit or loss. For example, the current year's forecast was prepared with three possible volume levels in mind. The budget reflects the varying costs and expenses according to each of the forecast levels, so that management can judge which course will be most profitable to pursue.

flexible hours (also called *flextime*)   A system allowing employees to select a daily work schedule other than the standard 9:00–5:00. The company may impose minimum standards, such as consistency of schedule, daily or weekly total hour limitations, and job coverage through coordination of flexible shifts.

Disadvantages include coordination between management and different staff members; the tendency for people to want frequent changes; and the difficulty of direct supervision. Advantages include escaping the commute period, being able to coordinate work hours with childrens' school hours or a spouse's work schedule, and improved employee morale.

float   The period between a transaction and the close of that transaction. Some organizations use the float to earn interest and use working capital during the period of payment and clearance. For example, deposits are made to the bank account late Friday afternoon and are not acknowledged until Monday. The bank has a three-day float on the funds. Or, checks are written on the 10th of the month, but the average clearance requires five days. The company may earn five days' interest on the funds until the checks clear.

floater   Insurance coverage added to an existing business policy, often to extend coverage to property purchased since initiation of the policy period.

floating debt   Short-term corporate debt that is refinanced on a revolving basis, such as commercial paper, lines of credit, or loans due in one year or less. Government floating debt includes Treasury bills and short-term notes.

floppy disk   A flexible storage device constructed of a thin layer of magnetic material on a piece of mylar, used to store information or programs. The floppy can be removed from the computer. In comparison, a hard disk is usually an internal part of the system, with limited, though large, storage capacity. Use of floppies expands that capacity.

flowchart   The diagram of steps in a program or procedure. One box is drawn for each step, and is connected to the preceding and following steps by lines or arrows. Different shapes may be used to indicate different types of operations to be performed. Some steps may be simultaneous, or the process may branch out because decisions are made at certain points.

The flowchart is usually vertical, with processes listed from top to bottom and decision points represented by loops and alternative reactions. A procedural flowchart may be vertical or horizontal. In the latter, processes move from left to right. Individual areas of responsibility can also be defined by placement of process steps vertically.

footnote   An important part of a financial statement, in which certain elements or components of the statements are explained or disclosed. Footnotes are also used to explain values or obligations not on the financial statements, such as contingent liabilities and obligations through lease contracts, past due accounts receivable or methods of inventory valuation, or current market value of real estate recorded at very low book value.

forecast   An estimate of sales in the future, usually for a one-year period. The forecast is part of the budgeting process, and should be based on reasonable and logical assumptions, in order to properly evaluate the actual outcome.

Example: One company that uses a field sales force developed its forecast on production per representative. When actual results varied from the forecast, individual sales representatives were identified as producing less than the average.

foreign corporation   A corporation whose domicile state is other than the one in which it is conducting business. To avoid confusion with corporations organized under the laws of another country, the term *out-of-state corporation* is often used in place of foreign corporation. *See* domestic corporation.

FPA   *See* Free of particular average.

free of particular average (FPA)   A marine insurance policy provision similar to the deductible provision found in other forms of insurance. Losses are paid above a specified level or percentage of total asset value.

frequency diagram   A statistical bar chart showing the number or frequency of events occurring or estimated to occur within a limited number of range groupings.

Example: The personnel department studies the salary range of employees in the organization. It prepares a frequency diagram showing the number of employees in each of six salary ranges. There is a direct relationship between salary range and the number of employees, which supports the contention of its study.

fringe benefits   A range of advantages offered by the employer as an inducement to employees beyond the salary level. Fringe benefits may equal or exceed 50 percent of salary and wage levels, making them a very important portion of total compensation. Benefits include various types of group insurance: health, life, and disability; paid vacations and holidays; free or low-cost counseling; membership; internal privileges, such as access to a coffee room; retirement plans; participation in company-sponsored events and discount programs; credit union; and tuition reimbursement.

full vesting   The condition an employee attains upon being eligible for 100 percent of benefits under terms of a retirement plan. Vesting may occur gradually over a period of months or years; or be achieved at the moment of qualification. When an employee is fully vested, he or she will receive the full value of the retirement plan upon reaching retirement age.

fully diluted   A theoretical value indicating the earnings that each share of common stock would earn if all warrants and options were to be exercised at the same time and all convertible bonds were converted. The calculation is valuable because it can be used consistently from one period to another, especially when some conversion does occur during one or more periods.

future value (also known as *accumulated value*)   The value of money in the future, if deposited at compound interest today. Future value will vary depending on the length of time involved, the compounding method used, and the interest rate. The "future value of 1" assumes a single deposit is made today and left on deposit to accumulate interest. The "future value of 1 per period" assumes that a series of deposits will be made over a period of time.

FY   *See* fiscal year.

G

GAAP *See* generally accepted accounting principles.

gap financing *See* bridge loan.

gateway A term used in computerized network systems. The gateway is a communications path leading from one system or network to another.

general journal One of three journals making up the books of original entry, the other two being cash receipts and cash disbursements journals. The general journal is used for all noncash, correcting, adjustment, and accrual journal entries.

general ledger The books of final entry, containing the permanent accounts and summarized transaction entries for balance sheet and income statement accounts. The usual arrangement of accounts in the general ledger is: assets, liabilities, net worth accounts, sales, direct cost accounts, expenses, nonoperating income, and nonoperating expenses. The general ledger is a summary document and should contain as little detail as possible. Details such as account analysis or breakdowns by customers or vendors are appropriately managed through subsidiary accounts or by worksheets. *See* subsidiary account; subsidiary ledger.

generally accepted accounting principles (GAAP) The collective rules, procedures, conventions, and standards under which accountants operate. The principles are developed and updated by the Financial Accounting Standards Board to provide accountants with consistent guidelines for valuation, interpretation, and reporting of financial information.

goodwill An intangible asset representing the assumed reputation value of a company, its product or service, or standing in the community or among its competition, often assigned at the time the business is sold.

gross margin   The percentage of gross profit (sales minus direct costs) to gross sales, used to compare results between periods.

group certificate   A document given to each participant in a group health insurance plan. The certificate spells out the contractual provisions of the group policy in very summarized form. More details and restrictions are explained in the master policy, which is usually kept by the employer.

group contract   An insurance policy that applies to a defined group (such as the employees of one company). The contract defines the group, spells out the terms and conditions of coverage, specifies benefits and maximum amounts, exclusions, and deductibles, and delineates eligibility requirements.

group disability   A group policy benefit that pays an eligible employee in the event of total or partial disability. Benefits are usually computed as a percentage of compensation, often 50 or 75 percent. The policy limits the length of time that group disability income will be paid.

group health   A health insurance policy issued to cover all eligible members of a defined group. The policy explains eligibility requirements, deductibles, benefits and their limits, and conversion privileges upon termination as a member of the group.

group life   A life insurance policy issued to all eligible members of a group, such as employees of one company. The amount of life insurance coverage per employee is often determined on the basis of annual income. Some group life policies include limited group disability benefits as well.

H

handicapped person   For employment law purposes, any individual who has either a physical or a mental impairment which limits life activity substantially; or has a history of impairment; or is thought to have the impairment. A handicap is defined as "substantially limiting" whenever it may cause problems for the individual in securing or keeping a job or advancing in a career.

hard copy   Output; the printed reports generated from a computer system versus what is seen only on the screen. One advantage to automation is the ability to *not* create more paperwork. A large volume of stored files may be kept in a very small space on the hard disk or on floppies and brought to the screen for reference at the convenience of the user.

hard disk   A storage unit for data that is usually constructed of metal and coated with magnetic material; or consisting of a series of storage chips. The hard disk is usually an internal part of the system unit, and is capable of storing a large amount of data, even in a very small computer. External hard disks can be added to the system for greater storage, often needed for multiple software programs. In modern applications, the hard disk has supplemented the floppy disk on many systems and is more common than in the past, when two floppy disk slots were used.

hardware   The machinery involved in a computer system. Operating instruments and programming languages, collectively called software, complete the system. The trend is toward development of systems that include hardware and software together, as well as hardware suited to software products and facilities from varying manufacturers.

hold harmless clause A contractual provision in which one side agrees to protect the other from liability of a specific nature, such as if certain claims are filed.

holding company A company that exists for the sole purpose of holding a controlling interest in the stock of other companies.

horizontal analysis A form of analysis involving comparisons in time, especially as applied to financial statements. The percentage of time from one period to another is studied, more so than the dollar values, as a means of determining how reasonable or predictable are the trends seen in current information.

horizontal selling A selling approach in which any and all buyers are considered as prospects, regardless of location. In comparison, vertical selling concentrates on a relatively small market segment.

hypothecation The use of an asset as collateral. When something is hypothecated, it is pledged without having to give up control or possession. In the event of a default, the creditor has the right to force sale of the asset or to take possession and title. For example, a company has a portfolio of securities, and borrows a large sum of money for twelve months, promising to repay it within that one-year term. The portfolio of securities is hypothecated as security for the loan.

hypothesis testing In statistics, determining whether a series of assumptions should be accepted. No matter how thoroughly a test is done, the basic premise might be flawed. Hypothesis testing enables the analyst to confirm or deny the assumptions before drawing conclusions.

I

impact ratio   In employment law, a calculation of the adverse impact in hiring, promotions, training, and other matters. To compute, divide the selection rate of the group in question by that of the group with the highest selection rate. *See also* adverse impact.

implied contract   A contract arising from actions or intentions of the parties, without written or oral agreement. Implied contracts may come into being when someone relies upon another, based on actions that create promises to perform or that lead the relying person to believe there is an agreement.

imprest petty cash   A fund set up to move cash payments through the books of the company, without needing to issue checks for small amounts. The fund is established in a fixed amount. As receipts are submitted, cash is paid out as reimbursement. At any time, the total of receipts, stamps, and cash in the fund should equal the fixed fund total.

   The imprest balance is established to take care of the cash-based needs of a company, department, or division. The amount should be great enough for that purpose, but small enough to require replacement at least once per month. At that point, all receipts are added up and coded, and a check is issued to replace the cash spent from the fund.

incentive pay   Compensation above salary in exchange for greater productivity or for achieving a specific result. Incentive pay requires reaching a level of performance and maintaining it for a period of time, such as the entire pay period. In comparison, a bonus is granted on a one-time basis and, if tied to performance, is achieved based on defined standards.

income replacement   The benefits to be paid under terms of a disability income insurance policy. The amount of insurance benefit is computed as a percentage of monthly income earned by the insured person, usually 50 to 75 percent. Because the benefit is not taxable, it is not necessary to replace 100 percent of gross monthly income.

income statement (also known as the *profit and loss statement*)   One of three commonly prepared financial statements, the other two being the balance sheet and the statement of cash flows (or cash flow statement). The income statement shows activity for a specified period, often a quarter or an entire fiscal year. It breaks down sales, direct costs, gross profit, expenses, net profit, provision for income taxes, and after-tax profit.

   The statement is often prepared on a comparative basis, showing results for both the current and the previous period. Income may also be reported with an accompanying breakdown of percentages, with gross sales representing 100 percent and all other lines reported as a percentage of sales. The percentage is usually listed to the right of the dollar figure. A comparative statement may also include percentages. This requires four columns, two for current (amount and percentage) and two for the previous period. A reviewer may then compare periods by amount as well as by percentage to gross sales.

indemnity   The payment of a claim or protection against loss. In property and casualty insurance policies, indemnity is designed to restore the insured property to the condition prior to the loss. Thus, the insurance should not improve conditions nor provide incentives to encourage or allow losses so that insurance is profitable to the insured.

independent event   In statistics, an event for which an outcome cannot be predicted on the basis of an unrelated event. For example, how does a business estimate gross profit and net income for a completely new product line, being marketed in a new region? Since there is no related event or history, the outcome is an independent event.

   To statistically reduce risks or forecast the near-term future, three steps are advised:

1. Draw a sample large enough to anticipate results of a larger body of events.
2. Be aware of changes as they occur in independent-event studies. Because no predictable comparison is available, early results might not indicate the overall trend.
3. Be prepared to modify test assumptions on a recurring basis. Update the test upon analysis of each new result, recognizing that the longer the study, the more accurate the estimate for an independent event.

indexing   A technique used to represent a larger body of information, when developing graphics. An index is a set value against which each value in a field is compared. The initial value is 100 (representing 100 percent), which may be the average period's outcome in the past, an assumed "typical" outcome, or the outcome considered a standard or ideal outcome.

   Given the value of 100 (percent), each value in the field is compared and represented on a chart above or below 100. One problem with indexing is that the assumed standard value might not be typical. If a field of values represents a changing trend, indexing may be very misleading; and the resulting line graph could distort rather than clarify outcome. The advantage of indexing is that it provides a simplified representation of the trend of a large body of information or relatively large values.

informal organization   The corporate culture, that element of interpersonal communication apart from the formal and highly structured operational culture. The informal organization includes friendships, alliances, and cliques. The strength and power of the informal organization are affected directly by the level of efficiency in the informal organization.

initial sale   The first sale to a customer who may be a likely future buyer. The initial sale is thought to be much more difficult than subsequent sales, so a measurement of initial sales can be used to forecast repeat sales volume. After the initial purchase, the customer is considered likely to return.

inland marine insurance   A specialized version of property and casualty insurance which includes protection against losses occurring during transportation of covered goods. Included are fire, theft, weather damage, derailment, and collision, as well as other named perils. *See* ocean marine insurance.

input **1.** The process of placing information in a computerized system. **2.** The body of data being placed into the system. Before the computer is able to process information, the information must first be entered via a keyboard, scanner, or modem.

intangible asset A noncorporeal asset. Some intangibles are listed on the balance sheet in certain cases, often upon sale of the business. Typical examples include a noncash covenant not to compete, assigned value of patents, and goodwill.

interface The connection between two or more components of a computer system or between networks. For example, the system unit interfaces with the keyboard, the display screen, and the printer. Remotely operated computer systems may communicate with one another through a modem, using a facility designed to collect and pass on electronic mail.

interim audit An internal or external audit conducted during the fiscal year rather than at the end. The purpose may be to present a certified statement for part of the year; to perform tests to reduce the year-end task to a degree; or to discover whether any immediate savings can be achieved. Interim audits in high-volume companies or divisions will cut down on the time required for a full-year audit at year-end, and may be undertaken to shift part of the workload away from the first quarter.

interim statement A financial statement prepared during the year, showing conditions and operating results for less than 12 months. Interim income statements prepared on a comparative basis should be for the identical period in the previous year. Balance sheets should be compared to the same date from the previous year.

internal audit An audit conducted inside the company, by employees in the accounting or internal auditing department. Internal audits emphasize keeping expenses under control and cash-oriented controls. The audit can identify control lapses and correct them, before they are discovered during an external audit. An external audit, in comparison, is designed to verify that the procedures in use are adequate and that the degree of control is acceptable. They test the files to determine that adequate records are being kept, as well as examine accounting decisions to test valuation methods.

internal control   A system aimed at providing employees with direct, hands-on control over transactions occurring in their department or area of responsibility. In comparison, an external control is one imposed from above or instituted as a matter of procedure.

internal rate of return (IRR) (also known as *discounted cash flow*)   A calculation used in investing and certain business applications. It assumes an established interest rate, to be applied to the time value of money and returns over a period of time.

For investors, the assumed rate of interest is what it is believed the investor could earn in outside investments. Thus, periodic cash flow is calculated on the basis of the present value of the assumed rate. In business applications, the assumed rate is an investment rate (for the business), often tied to historical percentages of net profit. In both instances, the assumed rate of return could be untypical in a changing investment or business environment. When IRR is used, the assumed rate should be applied consistently to all possible outcomes in the study.

Several different methods are used to calculate IRR, depending on the purpose. The simplest is to multiply each year's net income or loss by the present value factor, based on the assumed interest rate and compounding method. Use annual compounding to avoid questionable justification for use of more frequent methods.

Example: A newly opened division is forecast to experience losses during the first two years, followed by increasing profits over the followed three years. What is the internal rate of return, assuming 8 percent compounded annually? To calculate, (1) multiply each year's net profit or loss by the applicable present value factor. The factor will decrease for each year, so that the fifth year's factor is much smaller than the first and second years' factors. (2) Divide the net present value by the number of years, to estimate the average annual return.

interpolation   An estimate of interest rates, yields, and other factors. Interpolation is used in calculating bond yields and interest rate factors.

Example: The bank recently quoted your company a loan rate of 10.125 percent. Your book of compound interest factors shows the factors for 10.00 percent and for 10.25 percent. The interpolated factor is the average of these two rates.

Factors can be interpolated for rates not exactly halfway between known rates. First calculate the rate halfway; then perform a second calculation to weight the interpolated rate.

Example: You want to calculate the interest factor for 10.125 percent; but your book of factors provides only 10.00 and 10.50 percent. (1) Calculate the average between 10.00 and 10.50 percent; and (2) calculate the average between the factor in the first step (10.25 percent), and 10.00 percent. This will approximate the factor for 10.125 percent.

inventory Merchandise on hand for resale, or components for manufacture or conversion to finished goods. The inventory is valued at cost or at market, depending on the accounting method being used. It is considered a current asset on the assumption that it is convertible to cash within one year.

inventory turnover ratio A ratio comparing the cost of goods sold to the average inventory. The purpose is to demonstrate how efficiently inventory levels are controlled. If the level is too small, materials will not be on hand when customers demand them; and if the inventory is too large, then working capital will suffer as insurance and storage costs rise. Some companies compare sales to inventory to calculate the ratio. However, when inventory is shown on the books at cost and sales are on a marked-up basis, the ratio could be distorted, especially if the average mark-up shifts during the year. It is far more accurate to compare the cost of goods sold.

To compute, divide the cost of goods sold for the period by the average inventory level during the period. The result is expressed as a number of turns. The "average" inventory should be computed with the degree of fluctuation in mind. For example, if inventory is extremely high during the summer months and extremely low during the winter, it would be inaccurate to take two December 31 figures and average them. It would be more accurate to add quarterly inventory levels and divide by five (prior year-end plus the end of each of four quarters); or include each month-end inventory level and divide the total by 13 (end of last year plus one value for each of 12 months in the current year).

$$\boxed{\frac{C}{I} = T}$$

C = Cost of goods sold
I = Average inventory
T = Inventory turnover ratio

IRR   *See* internal rate of return.

J

job cost accounting A form of accounting in which costs and, often, expenses, are broken down in detail by job. It may be used in construction, engineering, and other industries in which sales and costs should be tracked and controlled on a per-job basis.

Some service organizations have attempted to apply job cost accounting in their environment. However, because service businesses have few direct costs, this attempt usually leads to arbitrary allocations—if the department is not able to control the expense level, there is no logical reason to perform allocations. Job cost accounting enables divisions or departments to directly monitor and control cost and expense levels, usually in a manufacturing and production environment. *See* allocation.

job description Documentation of the specific duties and requirements of a job. The document includes task descriptions with deadlines; sources of information; reports and forms; and other conditions of the job.

job evaluation Analysis of the jobs performed in a department or company. The purpose is to seek better ways to perform work, including elimination or consolidation of jobs or the creation of new jobs. Another function of job analysis is to determine and establish appropriate pay levels for a range of tasks performed within one job.

job related A condition directly related to the job the employee performs or will be expected to perform. The question of job relatedness is raised to determine whether or not a test can be fairly administered, or if the basis for adminstering the test is fair. For example, a company may require applicants for a manual labor job to pass a math test. However, the questions and answers are not job

related, so the company may not be legally able to administer the
test. If the position were for a cashier, however, a math test would
be completely proper, as it is job related.

job rotation   A system of moving employees between two or more
different jobs. This exposes employees to different skills and improves their point of view and skills. It also helps management to
provide coverage over several jobs and reduces the occurrence of
boredom among employees performing extremely routine tasks.

job sharing   A division of responsibility for one job between two
people. This occurs when jobs are eliminated: As an alternative to
terminating an employee, two are given part-time jobs; one works
in the morning, the other in the afternoon. Job sharing also arises
when workers want only part-time work, but the employer has a
need for a full-time staff.

K

keyboard   The point of input for a computer system. Most keyboards contain the same keys as the typewriter, with a numeric pad and a number of specialized command keys. Text and commands are communicated by typing, and the results can be reviewed on a screen.

key employee insurance   Life, health, or disability insurance on an individual partner or corporate shareholder. The company is the named beneficiary in the policy to protect it in the event of a loss (to life or health, for example) of the insured. The company would otherwise be unable to continue in operation or to afford to buy out the interests of the ill or deceased person. Benefits under the policy would pay medical bills or living expenses or, in the case of key employee life insurance, would be used to purchase the deceased person's equity.

kiting   The inappropriate borrowing or theft of funds, accomplished by moving money from one account to another to replace monies previously taken. For example, a check is improperly drawn on one business account and is shortly replaced by a deposit from another account. When a number of accounts in different banks are involved, the process may continue without being detected for many months, with the amounts involved steadily increasing.

Kiting and other forms of misappropriation are prevented through complete internal auditing and cash control procedures. Successful kiting depends on the time delays involved with clearance of checks between banks. As the banking system continues to employ electronic clearance procedure, kiting becomes less practical.

L

labor-intensive Descriptive of an activity in which the cost of labor is more of a factor than the cost of capital. However, the term is used widely to describe time-consuming projects even when capital costs are not an issue.

laissez-faire leadership Descriptive of a leadership style opposite of authoritarian. This leader provides as little as possible in the way of direct control and guidance to employees, although control may be achieved through less obvious means. This manager believes that employees excel if left alone to take responsibility for their own tasks. If employees respond well to this style, it is highly effective. Thus, the skillful laissez-faire leader carefully selects employees who are most likely to work best in that environment.

LAN *See* local area network.

lapping A technique used by embezzlers. A cash shortage is hidden by a delay in ordering receipts into the books. Lapping can be effective with only a one-day delay.

    Example: A bookkeeper is able to conceal an embezzlement with this technique: Cash is received on Monday and appropriated. On Tuesday, a second customer pays in cash, and the bookkeeper enters the needed amount in the first customer's account. The same process can be repeated from one day or week until the next. As of the monthly cut-off point, the customer left with the unrecorded payment will assume that credit will show up the following month, and it will.

    Lapping requires constant maintenance and, in most cases, the embezzler is caught. There is a tendency to increase the amount being moved around in the books, so that at some point it is no longer possible to hide the discrepancy.

lapse   The cancellation of an insurance policy due to nonpayment of the premium. A lapse may occur as a means of ending the insurance expense, as when a policy has been replaced with another; or it may be accidental. The company often will allow a lapsed policy to be reinstated if payment is made within a limited period of time. The company is aware, however, that the desire to reinstate may be a sign of adverse selection—the tendency to want insurance coverage when the individual knows a claim is pending, or when he or she is at greater than average risk.

last-in, first-out (LIFO)   A method of valuing inventory in which it is assumed that the last goods purchased or manufactured were the most recent ones sold. As a result of this assumption, the merchandise still on hand is valued at the oldest cost applicable. The effect of this method is to show less profit when prices are rising than does the alternative method, first-in, first-out. *See* first-in, first-out.

law of large numbers   A mathematical theory with applications in statistics and insurance. The law states two points: (1) The larger the sample used in a test, the greater the accuracy of any predictions made using the sample; and (2) the larger the sample used in a test, the less deviation to be expected in comparisons between outcomes.

In statistical applications, the law establishes the premise for estimating future outcomes, even using a very limited sample. An outcome based on a relatively small sample may be considered realistic or fair, as long as the law of large numbers is accepted and the sample is a fair representation of the larger population.

In insurance applications, actuarial calculations of mortality and other losses are used to establish premium levels. Under the law of large numbers, a fair estimate can be made of when losses are likely to occur. Thus, life insurance rates vary for each age. Similar applications are used for casualty and health insurance, based on actual loss experience.

LBO   *See* leveraged buy-out.

lease   A contract in which one person or company (the lessor) grants rights to another (the lessee) to use an asset. That asset is not sold, but the lessee does take possession and assumes responsibility for insurance and maintenance during the lease period. The lease payment is contractual, and the asset must normally be returned at the end of the term in acceptable condition. The lease may also specify conditions under which the leased asset may be converted and sold to the lessee.

leasehold insurance Casualty insurance for the lessor. In the event of loss, the policy reimburses lost income that would have been earned under terms of the lease. Benefits normally will continue as long as the property cannot be leased as a consequence of the loss.

legal entity A person or company that has legal standing in the eyes of the law. This includes adults and corporations, for example, which may enter into contracts, but excludes minor children, who are not legal entities and may not legally enter contracts.

legal purpose A concept of contract law stating that a contract is legal and enforceable only if it complies with public policy and the law. For example, a business agreement entered into for an illegal purpose is not a legally binding contract. Thus, a contract between two individuals or companies may be void or voidable if it contains provisions that do not conform to the concept of legal purpose.

letter of credit A written commitment provided by a bank or other institution stating that the bearer is authorized to draw a bill of exchange upon the letter, for a specified business purpose. It is a form of loan commitment, a contingent line of credit committed to by the lender. It also gives assurance to a supplier that the buyer or merchant is able to pay for goods to be delivered. The letter of credit is used widely in international trade where goods are transferred between countries, and shippers may be unwilling to proceed without assurances of the borrower's ability to pay. In such cases, an irrevocable letter of credit issued by the purchaser's bank guarantees payment for goods shipped, based on delivery of shipping documents.

letter quality Descriptive of a computer printer that produces print of a quality similar to that of a typewriter. Letter quality printers may be slower than dot matrix unless they are of the laser variety, in which case they may be of comparable speed. Many dot matrix printers have a mode called composition quality, which is so close to letter quality that only the shape of the letters indicates that output was produced by a dot matrix printer.

level debt service A form of loan repayment in which each month's payment is identical. This applies in most forms of loan, whether fully amortized or not. For example, a fully amortized loan is calculated at the level debt service required to retire the loan within a specified number of months or years, based on the amount borrowed, compounding method, and interest rate. Use of level debt service does not always mean the loan will be amortized over the indicated period. Many possible arrangements may be made. A loan may be amortized using level debt service for an extended period, but be due and callable within a shorter period, for example. Or level debt service may be mandated for interest-only payments, with the entire principal amount due and payable at the end of a specified period of months or years.

leverage   **1.** In general and in investing, the use of borrowed money to gain control over the largest possible number of properties and investments. **2.** In finance, the study of debt and equity in relation to one another, as a test of capitalization and the trend toward higher or lower debt financing. The purpose of such a study is to identify shifts from profits, which may be given to shareholders as dividends, to debt service, in which lenders receive interest. **3.** In administration and accounting, the degree to which expenses are fixed and predictable or variable. **4.** In general use, the acquisition and application of power and influence within the company. Leverage is used to assert political pressure, to win advantages, or merely to consolidate a political base for future use. The term may be interchangeable with influence.

leveraged buy-out (LBO)   The takeover of another company using leverage. Funds are borrowed and the takeover company's assets are pledged as collateral for the loan. From the point of view of the acquiring company or group, the loan should be repaid from operating capital of the newly acquired company. For example, a group of shareholders offers to take over control of the corporation. They receive a pledge of funds from a lender and offer a price per share of stock, promising to replace the current management with new managers. The plan calls for repayment of the loan from operating profits.

liability   A debt of the company. Liabilities consist of operating accounts payable and accrued liabilities; taxes payable; notes payable; and other debt obligations, such as long-term bonds.

Liabilities are divided into two broad categories. Current liabilities are due and payable within one year. In addition to all current accounts payable, this group should include 12 months' payments on notes and other debt contracts. Long-term liabilities are due in more than 12 months. The combination of liabilities and net worth is equal to the total of assets as reported on the company's balance sheet.

liability insurance   Insurance protection against losses to property or personal injury, due to conditions in the insured person's or company's control; or for damages awarded as settlement of a damage claim. Liability insurance protects against the economic consequences of a liability claim. Although the chances of such a claim may be minor, the company could not afford the contingent claim and needs the insurance protection in order to remain in business. *See also* business liability.

LIFO   *See* last-in, first-out.

line graph   A graph used to report trends and other forms of information that change over time. The line graph is designed to show singular or relative information and change. For example, monthly or quarterly financial information, transactions processed, units produced, or sales calls made are appropriate for reporting on a line graph. Each of these types of information is summarized in analysis and reports each month.

In most situations, the vertical side of the square or rectangular graph (the x axis) represents value (dollars, percentages, or numbers). The horizontal side (the y axis) represents time. The line graph usually has one value scale, although related information can be reported with two scales, one on the left side and the other on the right. This is appropriate when combined information is being compared on the same graph. For example, you might compare the number of units produced to the change in the percentage of defects over the same period of time.

Comparative graphs should use the same scale whenever possible to avoid unintentional distortions. Thus, when a report contains several different graphs for the same time period, and all are reporting in dollars, summarize information in graphs of identical size.

Scales should be spaced and reported evenly for the same reason, with the bottom value equal to zero (or, if some trending is reported below zero, the scale should be spaced adequately so that the shape of the graph is not overly distorted).

The line graph is effective for reporting two related trends (such as sales to direct costs). However, great care should be taken to keep the graph as simple and clear as possible. This is achieved through design, as well as clarity of title or legend. When reporting two related trends, use dissimilar symbols (such as solid and broken lines). Also clarify with annotation or footnote when required. *See* bar graph.

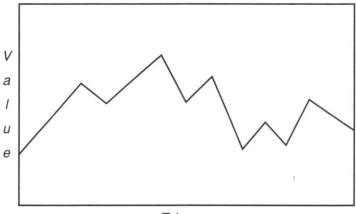

line of credit   A form of debt financing in which the company is given a credit limit it may use at its own will and for any purpose. In comparison, a loan is granted for a specific purpose in most cases and funds are delivered to the borrower as soon as approval and review are complete. The advantage of a line of credit is that funds are taken only when needed, which reduces interest expense. In addition, upon repaying the line already used, the company may take out the funds again, up to the limit of the line of credit. Repayment is required at minimum levels, although the entire amount drawn may be repaid at any time without prepayment penalty. The line may be cancelled and repayment demanded at any time. The line may also be extended upon request, if the lender approves the extension requested.

lines per minute (LPM)   A measurement of printer speed, when comparing extremely fast printers. In slower version printers, the usual measurement is CPS, or characters per second.

liquid asset   An asset in the form of cash or convertible to cash in twelve months or less. Examples include current accounts receivable, inventory, notes receivable, and marketable securities.

liquidity   The degree to which a company can convert its assets to cash without difficulty or financial loss. When cash is tied up in long-term assets, the company has a lower degree of liquidity. Current assets, including accounts receivable, inventory, and securities, are considered highly liquid.

loan commitment   A promise made by a lender to loan money to a company. The commitment usually includes the amount, the purpose of the loan, and the interest rate. It may also impose a deadline or indicate a time limit for the loan commitment, through which that interest rate and the commitment itself will apply.

loan value   The amount of collateral value a lender places on collateral and, as a result, is willing to lend. This is not a way of indicating lower value; it does limit the lender's risk, and sets a minimum equity level for the borrower.

   Example: A lender will loan up to 75 percent of appraised value of real estate. A company seeking financing owns a $1 million property. That property has a loan value of $750,000.

local area network (LAN)   A coordinated network of automated systems, in a limited geographical area, allowing communication between a number of computer users or systems within an affiliated group, or for a similar purpose such as sending and receiving electronic mail of a particular type.

logic   1. The pattern of orders and instructions in a computer program. A well-designed system consists of both logic and convenient sequencing of commands. 2. The operational procedures in hardware circuits.

long-term assets   Capital assets owned by a company, net of accumulated depreciation. These assets are called "long-term" to distinguish them from current assets (which are cash and other assets convertible to cash within one year); the term implies that the company will own them for many years. It is also assumed that long-term assets will hold their value for many years, in spite of the fact that book value declines as the result of depreciation. The classification includes all assets subject to depreciation, as well as the purchase value of land, which cannot be depreciated.

long-term goal   A goal that a company or individual plans to meet beyond the next twelve months. For example, an employee may set a series of short-term goals relating to the immediate future; and a long-term career goal based on experience, education, and time on the job. A department may state a long-term goal related to the nature of work performed for the company. And the company may set a long-term goal as part of its marketing and business plan, to gradually become influential in a new market, or by offering a new product or service.

long-term liability   Debt of a company that is due and payable beyond the next twelve months. Included in this classification are balances of notes and contracts except for the next twelve months' payments; and other long-term obligations, such as bonds and notes.

loss leader   An item advertised at an extremely low price, often at a loss to the company. The purpose is to attract customers to the retail location so that they may purchase other goods while there. A given percentage of those customers will buy something.

loss prevention   A concept in risk management, in which risks of loss are reduced as far as possible in order to (a) reduce the cost of insurance, or (b) avoid the need for outside insurance coverage. Installation of smoke alarms and removal of fire hazards, initiation of safety procedures and equipment, and implementation of normal maintenance procedures on equipment and motor vehicles are examples of loss prevention.

LPM   *See* lines per minute.

M

machine language   A computer language written in binary code, used for direct execution and internal communication within the computer itself.

magnetic disk   A floppy or hard disk with a coating of magnetic material, used in a computer to store information.

mail order   A form of sales in which advertising is aimed at the customer who will send in orders by mail. The order and the goods are mailed, and little or no direct contact occurs between the customer and a salesperson or sales staff. Mail order is more expensive initially than retail sales, for example, since a lot of capital is invested in advertising. However, it is less expensive overall, since the company is not required to support sales through fixed overhead and location expense.

mainframe   The largest grouping of computers, distinguished by the size of memory and processing power. Minicomputers and microcomputers are the smaller classifications.

management by exception (MBE)   A style of management in which employees are left alone to execute normal routines in a normal manner. If and when problems arise, the MBE system assumes that they will be brought to the manager's attention. Or, if the manager is not advised by someone else, it is generally assumed that he or she will respond to the problem through observation. Energy and emphasis may then be replaced on dealing with exceptions, rather than on routines that work without the manager's help. Proponents of this theory believe that only the exceptions need attention, and that managers should leave matters alone as long as exceptions do not arise.

management by objectives (MBO)   A style of management in which specific goals are defined and given a deadline. The manager and employees then agree to reach the targeted goals, and performance is monitored with those goals in mind. If necessary, the manager will take or direct actions required in order to meet the objective. With objectives defined, everyone works toward the same desired result. Supporters of this theory believe that the most important feature is the definition, and that without definition, there can be no goals and no coordinated action.

management information systems (MIS)   A series of routines, processes, and procedures aimed at providing management with crucial and timely information. MIS may be computerized tools to aid in decision making, analysis, and a range of forecasting or marketing functions. In modern applications, MIS means much more. It is the approach to providing information, rather than just programs designed to gather data and report.

marine insurance   *See* inland marine; ocean marine insurance.

marketing securities   Current assets that include investments readily convertible to cash. This may include stocks and bonds, money market funds and accounts, or shares of mutual funds. The company may purchase marketable securities as a temporary investment, to maximize the use of cash without investing in nonmarketable assets.

marketing concept   A theory of management which states that corporate goals are best met when methods are found allowing customers to meet their goals. The satisfied customer supports the company and its own goals.

marketing mix   The entire advertising, promotion, and marketing program. Included are budgets, staffing, expansion programs and plans, product features and pricing, merchandising and distribution systems, and the range of decisions made in these areas.

marketing plan   **1.** The specific strategies used to market the product or service. **2.** A business plan emphasizing the marketing changes or programs to be instituted in the coming year. The marketing plan may also be incorporated as part of the larger corporate business plan, and serves as the basis of assumptions used to develop the sales forecast, define current and future markets, and identify likely changes in the customer base.

market pattern   The comparative level of sales volume in one area or another, or in all areas; or the tendency in the overall market to buy or not buy a product. The market pattern is used to analyze the effectiveness of advertising and promotion, and also to emphasize products in specific regions. A market test may be aimed at making judgments about the market pattern, or estimating the trend and direction and what that might mean for the company's product.

market planning   *See* marketing plan.

market saturation   The point at which continuing sales may no longer be expected, due to decreased need, obsolescence, or a shortage of customers. In these conditions, the market is no longer generating new demand for the company's products or services.

market segmentation   The analysis of a market, broken down by demographic attributes, buying patterns, consumer behavior, or internal divisions (branch and sales offices, for example). Segmentation helps marketing executives compare similar regions and to test the effectiveness of different marketing strategies.

market theory   A theory stating that salary and wage levels should be determined primarily by supply and demand factors. In situations when a particular skill is in high demand and few people are available with that skill, the market theory states that compensation should be increased accordingly; and when a particular skill is more abundant than the demand, compensation should be reduced accordingly. Although the market theory cannot be realistically applied, it is a commentary favoring the pure theories of supply and demand, but as applied to the labor market rather than to products. To an extent, the market theory can be witnessed in a free economy. Scarcity of certain skills does lead to higher compensation. But when skills are abundant or can be replaced by cheaper technology or automation, the demand and the compensation both fall away.

master policy   The contract for group insurance issued to the employer or administrator. Each participating employee receives a group certificate which spells out the terms of coverage, but the master policy is the contract under which insurance is provided.

master-servant rule   A theory in agency law specifying that the principal (employer, for example) is legally responsible for the negligent acts of the agent or employee. The theory extends to the idea that the principal is responsible even when the specific acts of the agent are not known at the time they are committed. It is the principal's duty to supervise the agent, and to set standards and limits on actions and statements.

MBE   *See* management by exception.

MBO   *See* management by objectives.

mean   Average; the middle point in a distribution when evenly weighted. To calculate, (1) add up the values in a field, and (2) divide by the number of values.

Mean is commonly used in business applications for reporting financial trends and information. It is more common than other summaries of raw data, such as median and mode. The mean, or average, can be reported in several ways:

▪ *Simple average* is the most common and most easily understood. Each component of the distribution is assigned the same value in the calculation. So if the distribution contains six values, they are added together and then divided by six.

▪ *Moving average* is more complex. If the distribution contains six values, instead of calculating six fixed amounts, a series of calculations is performed over time. At each calculation point, the oldest value is dropped, and a new one is added. For example, a six-month moving average might begin with July through December and be reported in January. The following month, July's value is dropped and January's value is added.

▪ Moving average may be calculated using the *exponential method*. This cuts down on the calculation required, and is appropriate for use when an exceptionally large distribution is involved. The exponential method adds a degree of weighting to the latest values in the distribution. *See* moving average; exponential moving average.

▪ *Weighted average* assigns greater significance to some values in the distribution and less to others. The greater weight is usually assigned to the latest values, often on the premise that more recent information is more relevant than older information. Weighting can be done in a number of ways.

In one weighting system, the weight value is increased for each period. So in a six-month study, the oldest month would have a value of 1; and the latest month would have a value of 6. The total count is added and multiplied by the weighting factor, and the sum is divided by 21 (1 + 2 + 3 + 4 + 5 + 6).

Weight may be increased only for the latest month, two months, three months, or more. The actual weighting method used is a matter of personal choice, although ease of calculation should also be considered. The same weighting method should be used in reporting from one period to another, and should be applied equally to all instances in a study. A change in weighting method should be made to increase efficiency and accuracy, not to create a desired or predetermined result. *See* weighted average.

$$\overline{x} = \frac{x_1 + x_2 + x_3 + \ldots + x_n}{n}$$

$\overline{x}$ = *Mean*
x = *Value*
n = *Number of values*

median The exact middle value in a distribution, calculated so that one-half of the values are higher and one-half are lower. In odd-numbered lists, the median is the single, middle value. In even-numbered lists, it is the average of the two numbers at the middle.

Median has fewer business applications than average, although it may be more accurate in some instances. In a list contains exceptionally high values at the extreme ends, calculating mean, or average, will produce an unrepresentative result.

mediation Negotiation between two disagreeing parties, involving a neutral third party or mediator. Under arbitration, the third party may have the right to impose a binding decision, where as a mediator usually does not. Mediation may resolve many differences that would otherwise go to litigation, and is less expensive and less time consuming. Making use of the mediation process prior to filing suit may be a contractual requirement in many instances. *See* arbitration.

megabyte One million bytes.

memory   Permanent and working storage areas in a computer, often referred to for comparisons of power and size.

menu–driven program   A program that leads the user through processing and access steps with a menu of choices. The menu tells the user the range of functions that are possible, and may lead to submenus and back to a main menu. Help may also be available when the user does not understand the range of functions, or does not know how to execute a desired routine. A command-driven system, on the other hand, requires the user to input specific instructions without the benefit of a menu. For this reason, the menu-driven method is popular and easier to learn. The new user does not require extensive training nor understanding of the entire program. A well-designed menu leads the user through the steps without the need for outside materials or orientation. *See* command-driven program.

merit rating   A system of evaluating employee performance and job skills. Under the merit rating system, the employee is given points or ratings through the evaluation process. Salary or wage increases or promotions are given based on the degree of merit achieved during the evaluation period. Many employers support the merit rating system, as it establishes standards and a grading method. In less formal approaches and evaluation processes, each reviewer's standards are applied separately, with less definition.

microcomputer (personal computer)   A small computer, often containing one terminal and a relatively limited amount of memory, which uses a microprocessor for its central processing unit.

microprocessor   A single chip, the processing unit that forms the basis of the microcomputer.

middle–of–the–road leadership   Descriptive of a leadership style based on the desire to balance the employer's or the department's needs with employee morale. Managers strive for adequate performance of work that is demanded, while also trying to maintain employee morale at an adequate level. The middle–of–the–road leader may be willing to accept defects or errors to a degree in exchange for a relaxed atmosphere, less demanding work environment, and higher employee morale; and may be willing to compromise a standard for quality or response in exchange.

minicomputer   A medium-sized computer, larger than a microcomputer and smaller than a mainframe. With advances in technology, size distinctions are rapidly disappearing in the computer market. Generally, this range is assumed to be capable of supporting several hundred terminals, and may be the most likely size for support of a small to medium-size business operation.

   The minicomputer system may also support separate terminals performing different tasks while accessing the same data base. However, the greater the on-line activity, the more slowly the system will respond. The power of the system, the number of terminals connected at the same time, the nature of the tasks involved, and the design of the database determine the practicability.

minimum wage   The lowest amount of money per hour that an employer may pay under the law or union contract.

MIS   *See* management information systems.

mode   The value that appears most often in a list, or more than once. If more than one value meets this test, then the list is said to contain more than one mode.

   Business applications of this statistical test are limited. However, the determination of a "typical" sale could depend on calculation of mode rather than of mean or median. For example, a mail order business usually sells one item at a time. So in a study of buying trends for a particular item, what will constitute a "typical" sale? The mean will distort the facts, because purchase of more than one item is not typical. The median will also be distorted in some cases, for the same reason. However, the mode is the sales price of a single item, so that it does, in fact, represent the typical sale.

modem   Modulator-Demodulator, an instrument that transfers data from a computer mode to a communications mode, and then back. For example, a telephone modem is used to receive and send computerized information over telephone lines from one computer to another.

modification rate   (also called *merit rating*) An adjustment in the annual insurance premium, based on actual loss experience during a prior period. The rate may be increased or decreased, based on actual claims versus expected claims.

   Example: A business liability policy is written with a provision for a modification rate. At the end of the first anniversary year, the annual premium is billed at 93 percent of the contractual rate, reflecting a favorable claims history. In the second year, claims were higher than expected, so the annual premium was billed at 104 percent of the contractual rate.

monthly compounding   Compound interest based on twelve calculations per year. Monthly compounding involves calculation of a monthly interest rate, equivalent to one-twelfth of the annual rate. This monthly rate is then applied against the principal balance. It applies to savings accumulation as well as to debt amortization.

To calculate the monthly rate, (1) divide the annual rate (in decimal form) by 12. (2) Multiply the previous balance by this rate to calculate monthly interest.

Example: You have deposited $1,000 in a savings account yielding 6 percent interest, compounded monthly. The monthly rate is one half of one percent. To prove this, divide the decimal equivalent of the annual rate by 12 (months):

$$\frac{0.06}{12} = 0.005$$

To calculate each month's compound interest, multiply the monthly rate of 0.005 by the previous balance, as shown in the table below:

Month	Interest	Balance
		$1,000.00
1	5.00	1,005.00
2	5.03	1,010.03
3	5.05	1,015.08
4	5.08	1,020.16
5	5.10	1,025.26
6	5.13	1,030.39
7	5.15	1,035.54
8	5.18	1,040.72
9	5.20	1,045.92
10	5.23	1,051.15
11	5.26	1,056.41
12	5.28	1,061.69

In this example, the annual percentage rate is 6.169 percent. The effects of monthly compounding increase the nominal rate of 6 percent to reflect payment of interest on interest. *See also* compound interest.

motivation research   Research conducted to anticipate probable consumer buying patterns and responses to products, product labeling, and promotional ideas.

moving average   The average, or mean, or a field of values that changes over time. A moving average tends to even out momentary distortions, enabling the analyst to spot long-term trends without being distracted by seasonal or unusual changes in the pattern of data.

   Example: A 12-month moving average begins with a calendar year, extending from January through December and reported in the following January. In the second month, the oldest value (from the previous January) is dropped, and the newest value (from the most recent month) is added. A new average is then calculated.

   The moving average may be weighted, so that the latest values are given more significance than older ones. This is done on the premise that the latest information is more significant than older information. Thus, it is appropriate to add weight to most recent data.

   Example: In a 12-month list, the last three months are counted twice, and the whole average is divided by 15 rather than by 12. Or, weighting is increased one count per month over the entire distribution.

   One method of weighting the moving average is the exponential method. This is a simplified calculation of moving average that automatically adds a degree of weight to the most recent outcome while reducing the math for each monthly calculation. The exponential method is practical when dealing with a large distribution of values and time. *See* exponential moving average.

multiple perils   A form of insurance coverage in which a number of different losses are covered under the terms of a single policy. This form of coverage is practical when one company has a number of insurance coverage needs, but desires to include them in a single series of payments rather than in payments for each policy on its own.

multiple pricing   The offer of two or more units of a product for a single price. For example, a product sells for 89 cents. The multiple pricing offer may be made as two for $1.70. The eight cents savings is a buying incentive. This is commonly practiced in both retail and mail order sales.

multiple retirement ages   A provision in certain retirement plans allowing eligible participants to choose a retirement age from a number of ages. The benefit level changes based on the option selected. For example, normal retirement age may be the earliest age at which the employee is allowed to retire. Deferred retirement ages may involve increased benefits, depending on the rules of the plan.

mutual assent   A theory in contract law stating that a contract is valid only if both sides agree as to terms and conditions in the agreement. There must be a meeting of the minds, or the contract does not exist.

N

natural business year   The 12-month cycle that a business experiences, which may not necessarily be the same as the calendar year. The natural business year often ends with the highest volume of the year and, at its conclusion, the lowest inventory levels. For many businesses, the natural business year is selected as the fiscal year as well. For example, a contractor's natural business year ends with the last month of summer. That is the highest volume month, but it ends with virtually no materials left in inventory.

natural group   A group that shares an attribute in common, for the purpose of qualifying as a group for insurance coverage. The group must exist in this manner or group insurance cannot be issued. However, the need for a common element is not difficult to meet. The employees of one company are a natural group. Private group insurance, sold to self-employed people, defines a group as the employees of the firm or the members of the self-employed person's family. Insurers also require that the group remain in existence for a specified period of time before qualifying for group insurance.

negative working capital   A situation in which the company's current liabilities are greater than its current assets. As a minimum standard, current assets are expected to exceed current liabilities by a ratio of 2 to 1. When the ratio falls below 2 to 1, it is an initial danger signal. When working capital is negative, the situation is extreme. It could indicate that the company should expect to have problems in the near future paying current bills and may not be able to continue operations at present volume levels.

nepotism   The practice of hiring relatives and granting them special consideration or privileges within the organization. Relatives may be given important positions, higher than justified compensation, or rapid promotions; or they may hold power because of their relationship to high-placed shareholders or officers.

net assets (also called *net worth*)   The net of a company's total tangible assets, less its total liabilities.

net income   Income earned after deducting all costs and all expenses from sales. *Net* has different meanings to different companies. It is important to make distinctions before comparing one company or one period to another. In some instances, nonoperating income and expenses are included in net income. In other cases, the net amount may be a pretax figure or an after-tax version of net profit. Depending on nonoperating income and expenses and on the amount of tax liability, the differences can be significant.

net interest expense   A company's interest expense, less its interest income. When both interest income and expense are included as non–operating adjustments on the income statement, the net expense may be shown on the expense side. The alternative is to show income and expense separately.

network   A system containing two or more computers and other connected devices, including modems, terminals, and communications systems.

net worth   The owner's book value and ownership in the business. It is the net of all assets minus all liabilities. The net worth section of the books includes several accounts: capital (in a corporation) or owner's equity less owner's draw (in a sole proprietorship or partnership); additional paid-in capital; and retained earnings (in a corporation) or profit and loss (in noncorporate forms of organization).

At the end of each year, the books are closed and the net profit is added to retained earnings (in a corporation) or profit and loss (other forms). Thus, all income, cost, and expense accounts are reduced to zero before the new year begins; and all balance sheet accounts continue with their balances forward.

nominal rate   The stated annual rate of interest, which is not necessarily the full yield. The nominal rate does not indicate the annual percentage rate, which will vary based on the compounding method in effect.

Example: An investment's yield might be described as 6 percent. Semiannual compounding will produce a yield of 6.09

percent; quarterly compounding equals 6.14 percent; and monthly compounding yields 6.17 percent. In each case, the nominal yield is 6 percent.

noncompete agreement   *See* covenant not to compete.

nonqualified plan   A retirement or incentive plan not qualified for tax deferred treatment under the current tax regulations. In such a plan, the employer is not subject to the rules defining discrimination and may have greater flexibility in design of the plan. However, the tax benefit of a qualified plan is lost. The freedom to favor employees who are more highly compensated may be of greater value to the employer than the tax benefits of deducting contributions to a qualified plan.

nonrecurring charge   An extraordinary item that appears on the company's income statement. It will not recur in the future and, accordingly, is mentioned and explained in a footnote. Examples include casualty losses, judgments, losses arising from foreign exchange fluctuations, large thefts, or changes in inventory valuation methods. The footnote section of the financial statement is one of the most important, since nonrecurring charges are explained there.

When statements are prepared comparing one period to another, nonrecurring charges should be deducted from both periods. Otherwise, the comparison will be distorted. Removal of nonrecurring charges may not occur on the formal statement itself; the exceptions must be explained by footnotes. However, in analysis outside of the statements, removal of nonrecurring charges in all periods is a requirement for accurate analysis.

normal distribution   The statistical result of a probability test, in which the range of outcomes is symmetrical. If placed on a graph in which possible outcomes are listed from top to bottom and the number of chances occur from left to right, the normal distribution takes on a bell shape. The number of outcomes rises in the middle, representing the most frequent or likely outcome; exceptions or remote outcomes will occur at the extreme right and left.

normal retirement age   The age at which an employee is expected to retire. For retirement plan purposes, normal retirement age must be attained before the participating employee can receive full benefits. This age is usually measured through two tests. First, a specific age must be reached; second, a minimum number of employment years must have been completed. In many plans, the employee may retire at this age, elect to continue working beyond that age, or accept reduced benefits for earlier retirement.

notes payable A liability for borrowed funds, which should be broken down into two groups: current notes payable is the sum of the next 12 months' payments; all amounts beyond that are long-term notes payable. *See* accounts payable.

notes receivable An asset representing amounts due from others under the terms of a promissory note. This account is distinguished from accounts receivable, which are due from customers, often on a revolving basis. Notes receivable are normally listed as current assets. *See* accounts receivable.

null hypothesis The beliefs and assumptions applied in the conduct of a probability study.

Example: The company's management believes that consumers will purchase more goods if they are packaged in smaller boxes. An alternative hypothesis includes the belief that, in fact, consumers will buy more if goods are packaged in larger boxes. In order to test the null hypothesis and the alternative hypothesis, a limited study is undertaken and the results reviewed.

See alternative hypothesis.

O

objective   A statement, usually about one paragraph long, that explains the company's purpose, ideals, standards, and mission. The objective statement should clarify and describe the company's product or service, its resources (internal staff, for example), and standard for quality or customer service. The objective is used as a guiding principle in setting companywide or departmental goals, establishing whether an expansion plan is timely and appropriate, and helping to ensure that the company's employees are working together and for the same purpose.

obsolescence   Loss of value due to factors other than physical deterioration or damage. An asset becomes obsolete for a number of outside factors, including:

- *Economic*—A faster, cheaper alternative becomes available, so that older machines or processes no longer can be operated efficiently.
- *Replacement*—Equipment that must be maintained becomes more expensive with time. The rate of replacement and related down time may render an asset obsolescent. Or, the manufacturer may cease to provide replacement parts and service expertise.
- *New technology*—Many older processes and machinery are replaced not by newer models but by alternative processing methods. An example is the replacement of manual typewriters with electric; and of electric typewriters with word processors. As new technology becomes affordable and widespread, old methods and machines become obsolete.

ocean marine insurance   Insurance covering losses to goods during transport by water. Included are losses from piracy, fire, sinking or capsizing, jettison, theft, and other liabilities. Most ocean marine policies exclude losses from dampness, mold, decay, wear and tear, and acts of war.

off–balance sheet items   Assets or liabilities not reflected on the company's balance sheet. The financial statements in common use may accurately reflect conditions but often fail to disclose material values. This is because financial statements are prepared in a uniform and conservative manner. Any nonbook values are excluded intentionally, so that interpretation cannot distort true values. Examples of off–balance sheet items include contingent liabilities, such as unsettled claims and judgments; liabilities committed under a lease contract; and the current market value of real estate not shown in the depreciated net value on the books. Such adjusting items are normally explained in footnotes.

   Example: A company owns its own headquarters building, which it purchased about 10 years ago at a cost of $250,000. The building was valued at $200,000 and land at $50,000. Book value has been reduced by $72,700, which is depreciation claimed over a 10-year period. The net value of building and land today is $177,300. However, a recent appraisal placed market value of the building at $525,000, a difference of $347,700. This difference is explained in a footnote as an off–balance sheet asset.

omitted dividend   A dividend that was scheduled but not voted by the board of directors. The reason may be financial problems of a temporary or permanent nature; or a belief in the minds of the directors that cash can be better used to fund operations than to pay dividends.

on-line   Systems, equipment, and input processes operating under a central processing unit's direct control. The user in an on-line system is able to review information in the database interactively; thus, updating, changing, adding, and deleting information is efficient and immediate. In comparison, data in an off-line or remote processing system is processed and checked, and then merged with a database.

on-the-job training   Hands-on training of new or transferred employees. This methods assumes that productivity may be achieved, although at a reduced level, during training; and that employees learn and retain more through on-the-job training than they would in a remote environment, such as a classroom. In certain environments, on-the-job training is not only more efficient, it is also less costly and less time consuming.

operating profit (also called *net operating profit*)   The net amount when direct costs and operating expenses are subtracted from sales. Excluded from the operating profit or loss are all nonoperating items, such as cash shortages, capital gains and losses, interest income and expense, foreign exchange rate gains or losses, and provision for federal income taxes:

Sales	$1,200,000
Less: direct costs	718,623
Gross profit	$ 481,377
Less: operating expenses	379,944
Operating profit	$ 101,433
Plus: nonoperating income	8,400
Less: nonoperating expenses	− 12,104
Pretax profit	$ 97,729
Less: provision for income taxes	32,251
Net profit	$ 65,478

operating system   Programming controls combined with a series of specific programs that together control, coordinate, and manage hardware. All hardware systems require operating systems in order to function.

opportunity cost   The theoretical best use of available capital. The projected yield from the project involving a large amount of capital is compared to what would be earned if the same money were invested in the highest yielding vehicle available now.

oral contract   A contract that is not in writing. In most instances, oral contracts are entirely legal and enforceable, but the terms of the actual agreement might be difficult to prove. Some forms of contracts must be in writing in order to be legal, such as contracts for the sale of real estate.

organizational capital   Capital used to build a company at the time it is initially organized. This is distinguished from developmental capital and operational capital, often for the purpose of raising debt or equity capital. Organizational capital is required for the period of time from commencement of activity until outlets are available for the generation of sales revenues or until such revenues begin coming in.

organizational culture The rules of behavior, customs, rituals, and implied treaties that govern actions and attitudes within the company. Most of these issues and rules are unwritten but all employees know of them and understand the need to observe them. Organizational culture changes very slowly, if at all, in response to a developing influence which emerges as new generations of employees replace older ones and as lower-ranked employees gradually are promoted.

organizational expense (also called *organizational cost*) The expense of getting a business ready to open its doors. Organizational expenses include improvements as well as expenses that would normally be considered operating expenses. They are not deducted as current expenses because they are incurred before the operation is a going concern. Organizational expenses are set up as assets and amortized, usually over five years or more.

Example: A company plans to open its doors at the beginning of the month. However, it is currently spending money on advertising and leasehold improvements. The owner has recently hired the company's first employee. Upon opening the doors, the employee will be a sales clerk. For now, he is helping to get the store ready. All money being spent now, except for the purchase of inventory for resale, is considered as organizational. It will be booked as an asset and amortized over 60 months from the date the doors are opened to the public.

organization chart A chart showing the chain of command for the organization, either by title or by name of the individual. In most organization charts, the stockholders and board of directors are at the top; then the CEO and president's names are listed; then the top and middle executive layers are given. Most large company organization charts stop at the individual level; and most medium-size companies stop at the departmental level.

original cost The basis in property owned by a company, used to determine the dollar value of a loss that an insurer will pay. Under the actual cash value system, depreciation is calculated based on the age of items lost and an assumed useful life and replacement value.

Losses are paid at current value less depreciation. Under the replacement cost system, the full replacement cost is paid upon establishment of a loss. However, even a full replacement cost policy may limit the amount of payment. For example, one company places a ceiling on claims equal to 400 percent of actual cash value, as calculated under that form of coverage. *See* actual cash value; replacement cost.

outcome   The result; a statistical event within a range of possible events, which may be judged by comparison to those events. In business statistics, the range of possible outcomes is one method for forecasting and for identifying risk. When the company is embarking on a new marketing plan or placing a new product on the market, for example, the risks are better understood when outcomes are estimated in advance. A relatively narrow band of most likely outcomes describes the probable risks the company faces; outside of that band, other outcomes are also possible.

output   **1.** Reports, lists, and other printed information from a computer system; or information transferred from one system (output) to another (input). Output, when consisting of printed material, is also referred to as hard copy. **2.** Productivity. Output in a manufacturing environment, for example, is measured as a means for determining how efficiently work is being performed. Production of defect-free units is one popular means for judging output. In nonmanufacturing environments, other means are devised to measure output.

overhead (also called *general and administrative expenses)*   The fixed expenses of a company. Overhead is distinguished from variable, or selling, expenses in that the expenses in this group do not vary as a direct result of intermediate changes in sales volume levels. However, overhead must be expected to increase as a consequence of significant expansion.

   Example: A company budgets its fixed overhead expenses from one year to the next, and no changes are expected. Last year, however, due to rapid expansion, the company moved its headquarters to a larger facility, hired more administrative employees, and incurred many additional expenses it did not have before. In this case, expansion moved fixed overhead expenses to a higher plateau of commitment. On that plateau, overhead should not vary significantly.

overtime   Hours worked beyond the normal or agreed-upon work week. Employees paid on an hourly basis are compensated for overtime by most employers at one and one-half times their usual hourly rate. In some cases, especially for working on holidays, the contract may involve double-time, or pay equal to 200 percent of the usual hourly level. Overtime rules generally apply to wage-earners who are paid hourly, or to those with salaries up to a specified level or at a specified ranking in the department. Supervisors and managers are usually exempt from the overtime pay system, but may be given compensating time off for overtime hours.

P

packaged software Software developed for general application, and containing no customized features. Packaged software, because it is uniform, allows little flexibility. The user is required to operate within the confines of the generalized design. Today, packaged and customized software are both becoming obsolete. These are essentially systems and procedures in automated form that can be tailored to a wide variety of uses.

partial vesting Vesting at less than 100 percent of a retirement account's full value. If an employee terminates prior to 100 percent vesting, the partial percentage is applied as the basis of future retirement benefits to be paid. In such cases, the vested percentage is payable to the employee upon reaching normal retirement age.

participating preferred stock A special class of preferred stock that provides stockholders with extra privileges. In addition to receiving a dividend based on earnings, participating preferred stockholders may be entitled to an extra dividend under certain circumstances.

participative management (also called consultative management) A form of management in which everyone is encouraged to take part in decision making, rather than the more traditional method, in which management and subordinate roles are clearly distinguished from one another. The idea of teamwork, employee participation, and experimental variations of management style come and go in various fads. In the 1960s and 1970s, quality circles were a popular and widespread representation of participative activity, although they were not touted as management as much as employee control and influence over their own work environment. Quality circles are still in use today in many companies, notably in manufacturing environments.

partnership   A form of organization in which two or more owners share the equity of a business. They may be active partners, involved in the day-to-day management and decision-making process; or they may be silent partners, providing capital but remaining out of the operation of the business. Partners may comprise several forms of organization, including individuals, corporations, or other partnerships.

   Example: One partnership has five partners. Two are self-employed individuals, one is a separate partnership, and the last two are corporations. Each of the five is considered a partner in the partnership organization.

passed dividend (also called *omitted dividend*)   A dividend that was not voted by the board of directors, even though it is normally paid. This may occur for any number of reasons, including current financial restrictions or problems, or the board's desire to apply profits in strengthening and expanding operations. For example, a company that has always declared and paid a quarterly dividend in the past is experiencing cash flow problems and slower than expected sales. The board does not vote the dividend this quarter; it is omitted, or passed.

payout ratio   A ratio applied to determine the trend between dividends on common stock and net income after payment of dividends on preferred stock. To calculate, divide the dollar value of dividends paid on common stock by the net income minus dividends paid on preferred stock. The result is expressed as a percentage. *See also* dividend payout ratio for the calculation's formula.

payroll account   A checking account established for the specific purpose of paying all expenses related to payroll. These include payroll checks, tax deposits, and quarterly or annual payments to state and federal governments. It is necessary to establish a separate account under some service agreements, in which an outside company uses the account to generate checks; and upon submission of a report showing the periodic payroll activity, the company transfers funds to cover the total current payroll expense. In other instances, the use of a payroll account is convenient for management or for the accounting department.

PC   *See* personal computer.

penetration   **1.** The degree of effectiveness of an advertising campaign in reaching the target audience. Penetration may be measured in terms of the percentage of households or consumers who own similar products in a specific area. **2.** The number or percentage of individuals, consumers, or homes in a test area that meet the terms of one or more testing mechanisms. For example, if 97 percent of all households in one area have television sets in the home, then advertising through television has a 97 percent penetration.

percentage-of-change graph   A graph that shows the degree of change rather than actual value in a series of outcomes. This is an appropriate technique in many instances, especially when small deviation from a normal or accepted level may be expected. For other trends, however, it may be deceptive, especially if recipients usually receive reports showing actual values in graphic form.

To calculate, divide the latest value by the previous value.

percentage-of-completion accounting   A method of accounting often used in contracting companies. A job's revenues and costs are booked according to the degree of completion of the overall job, which is usually calculated based on direct cost expenditures at a given point. When income is received prior to the relative percentage, it is deferred until earned. When income is earned but the cash has not yet been received, it will be accrued and reported in the current year. Percentage-of-completion is more accurate than completed contract accounting for reporting long-term contract income. Under that method, no income or costs are booked until the entire project is complete. Thus, at year-end, a significant amount of profit could fail to be reported on the books because the job was not 100 percent complete. This is a distortion, since a percentage of that profit will have been earned as of the end of the year. *See also* accounting method.

percentage-of-sales method   A budgeting method for marketing expenses, in which the budget level is expressed and computed as a predetermined percentage of the forecasted dollar level of sales. This is preferred by many marketing and advertising departments, where success is measured in terms of increased revenues. The argument is that growth in volume is the direct result of marketing efforts. Thus, in order to continue successful expansion of markets, products, and customers, the budget should be treated as a direct cost or variable expense.

per diem   Literally, "by day," a system of pay or allowance based on a daily level. This is applied most often to travel, where a meal allowance is given or spending limited on a per diem basis. Employees may also be paid for per diem work.

performance appraisal   Evaluation of an employee's performance to determine pay raises or promotions. In this system, the supervisor or manager evaluates performance against specific criteria. For example, the supervisor and employee may agree in advance that during the coming six months, the employee will master the department's computer system. At the end of the six-month period, the employee's mastery of the system is evaluated. Proponents of this procedure recognize that the employee can excel once a specific goal has been established; without a goal there is no logical or equitable method for appraising performance.

per inquiry advertisement   A method of advertising in which the owner of the medium (usually a magazine or periodical) is compensated not on a space fee, but based on the number of inquiries resulting in completed sales.

periodic inventory method   *See* perpetual inventory method.

permutation   The number of different ways that an outcome may occur, regardless of the order of occurrence. The formula is used in statistics to identify the possible outcomes in a range.

$$^n p_r = \frac{n!}{(n-r)!}$$

n = *Number of factors*
p = *Permutations*
r = *Number of arrangements*
$!$ = *Factorial*

perpetual inventory method   (also known as *continuous inventory* or *periodic inventory method*)   A system of counting inventory in which the count is maintained on a continual basis. The book value of inventory is changed periodically to reflect changes in the physical inventory.

personal computer (PC) A machine for home, office, or hobby use, and the smallest classification of computers. As technology improves the efficiency of smaller computers, a growing number of business applications are available on the PC. These smaller computers may also be used to process and store a limited amount of data remotely and transfer it to a larger office system.

personal selling Selling in person, through face-to-face contact rather than through the mail or over the telephone. Although personal selling may be more time consuming and fewer consumers are contacted, supporters believe that a higher ratio of completed sales results from personal selling; and that personal loyalty creates more long-standing, repeat customers than do direct mail and other remote methods.

petty cash fund A cash fund established, usually at the departmental level, for reimbursement of incidental employee cash expenses. The fund is kept by one person, who periodically adds up and codes expenses and submits a check request to the bookkeeping or accounting department. The check is cashed and proceeds are used to replenish the fund to its full balance.

pie chart *See* circle graph.

planned obsolescence A concept in marketing that builds and times a permanent future market. The product is so designed that it has a finite useful life. During that useful life, the product is manufactured and offered to the customer. At the end of the useful life, the product is rendered obsolete by introduction of a different, improved product, an upgraded version of the old product, or the announcement and release of cheaper or more efficient technology. The consumer feels compelled to buy the replacement product, since the first purchase is then obsolete.

plotter A form of printer using pens, often of several different colors, used to create graphs from computerized programs.

population In statistics, the complete body of information, facts, or numbers that will be subjected to a study. The study will be confined to only part of the whole population, which is called the sample. It is practical to select a representative sample, but rarely possible to test the entire population.

Example: A food manufacturer wants to test a new product it is considering offering to the public. Testing is performed in several cities, and is limited to 1,000 attempts. The sample is believed to be representative of reactions among the entire population.

positioning   1. A judgment of the consumer's perception of a product's value and benefit, compared to other, competing products. The manufacturer of a product hopes to create the best possible positioning for its product. **2.** The location of advertisements in printed media or of a commercial in a radio or television program. Some positions, such as on a right-hand page or centerfold, or during prime time, are considered far more valuable than others and are priced accordingly.

power of attorney   A document or instrument which, by appointing a person as agent, grants that person the right to act in behalf of another, as well as to perform specific acts or types of acts on behalf of the principal.

preferred stock   A form of stock that is generally for the most conservative of equity investors. In the event of liquidation, preferred stockholders are given priority of claim over the company's assets, before claims of the common stockholders.

premium   1. An incentive offered to a buyer, either at a reduced price or free, to purchase a product or item. **2.** An additional charge or payment given or asked in exchange for consideration. For example, a magazine may increase its normal advertising rate when a company wants to specify placement and positioning of its ad in the magazine. Or, a company may charge an additional handling fee to meet an accelerated delivery deadline for a customer. **3.** A price above face value. This term is used most often to describe bonds which, because their interest rate is fixed at an attractively high level, hold a current market value above 100 percent of the face value. For example, a $1,000 bond at a premium of 103 has a current market value of $1,030.

prepaid expenses (also called *prepaid assets*)   An asset account used to report unamortized balances of certain expenses.

Example: A company makes a single payment for casualty insurance. The coverage period is 36 months. The amount of the payment is coded into the prepaid insurance account; and one thirty-sixth is removed each month and transferred to the insurance expense account.

presentation   A face-to-face report or show, often including carefully planned visual aids. In advertising, presentations are made to clients to gain approval for new campaigns. In business applications, presentations are made during sales pitches or internal meetings, for example, and may include handouts, slides, and sample materials.

present value   The value today of a future sum of money, assuming a rate of interest, a compounding method, and the number of months or years that compounding occurs. Present value is greater when the interest rate is higher, when compounding occurs more frequently, and when time extends further.

  The "present value of 1" is the value today of a sum of money that a deposit of one dollar will grow to in the future. It is based on the assumption that a single deposit would be made today. The factor from a present value table for one dollar is multiplied by the target amount to arrive at the required initial deposit. The "present value of 1 per period" is the same value, but it is based on the assumption that a series of regular deposits will be made, beginning today and continuing throughout the period in question. The factor for one dollar per period is multiplied by the target amount, and the answer is the amount of periodic deposits required to be made.

pretax profit   The net profit earned by the company after allowing for all income, costs, and operating and nonoperating income and expense but before deducting a provision for federal income taxes; the bottom line before allowing for federal income tax liability. *See* after-tax profit; operating profit; net income.

preventive maintenance   Scheduled routines to keep machinery in running order, to prolong the life of an asset and to save money by avoiding more costly repairs and reduce the need for more capital investment for the company. Responding after breakdowns have occurred or when symptoms of trouble first appear results in higher costs and more frequent down time.

price/earnings ratio (P/E ratio)   A stock's current market price divided by the most recent earnings per share. If earnings per share from the last year is used, it is a trailing P/E; if earnings per share as calculated by an analyst is used, it is a forward P/E. The P/E ratio is widely used by analysts to judge a stock's popularity and volatility. However, it is a controversial ratio, and analysts do not always agree on its value or on how to interpret it. One problem is that current market value may change daily, and does not necessarily reflect real fundamental values; earnings per share can be either out of date or based on current estimates.

$$\frac{M}{E} = R$$

M = Market price of stock
E = Earnings per share
R = p/e ratio

primary earnings per share A calculation of net earnings available to common stockholders. Net earnings after deducting federal income taxes is further reduced by dividends payable to preferred stockholders. The balance is then divided by the number of common shares outstanding.

$$\frac{N - T - P}{S} = R$$

N = Net earnings
T = Federal income taxes
P = Dividends on preferred stock
S = Number of common shares outstanding
R = Primary earnings per share

primary marketing area The main region where products are sold or, particularly in service industries, the primary customer or client. For example, a financial services company may consider wealthy professionals as its primary marketing "area," since they are more likely than most other consumers to need a given product or service and be able to afford it.

printer The machine used to print output from a computer. Dot matrix, letter quality, and laser jet are three main types, with a large range of variations to each. Serial printers will print one character at a time, with speed measured in characters per second. Line printers print an entire line at a time, and speed is measured in lines per minute. Printers may also be used to produce graphics or very high-speed output. Modern printers may be programmed so that instructions are fed back to the computer, rather than the other way around. In some cases, the degree of programming is so sophisticated that printers direct computers during printing operations.

probability   The likelihood that one or more outcomes will occur, given the range of possible outcomes. In one respect, probability is the opposite of statistics. Probability is the study of results when a process is understood, and statistics provides the likely result when the process is not quite as certain.

probability space (also known as *sample space*)   In statistics, the range of possible outcomes in a set.

problem-solution advertising   A form of advertisement in which a commonly understood problem is posed in the form of a question or description of a problem. The question is then answered or solved in the ad or the product is offered as a solution to the problem.

product differentiation   Distinctions between products, either real or imagined, when the products are approximately the same in value and quality. The distinctions may be emphasized in methods of packaging and advertising, quality, design variation, or performance or delivery claims. Such practices are most common in consumer goods industries.

product life cycle   A concept in marketing stating that some products undergo a natural life cycle, from introduction through expiration. During the earlier phases of the life cycle, sales are generated on a trial basis. In the later phases, purchases level off and then diminish as consumers begin trials with newer products.

professional liability insurance   Insurance protecting professionals against losses. For example, accountants, attorneys, physicians, and dentists have high exposure to malpractice losses; malpractice coverage is a form of professional liability insurance.

profitable volume   Descriptive of newly generated sales volume that also increases gross profits and net profits, on a permanent basis. Unprofitable volume, in comparison, with lower gross margins and higher operating expenses, results in lower profits. Companies may judge and control their expansion programs by identifying the steps needed to generate profitable volume; and to reverse trends which demonstrate that unprofitable volume is being allowed.

profit and loss account   An account in the net worth section of an unincorporated business, in which the year's net profit or loss is closed. As of closing, the sum of all asset, liability, and net worth accounts is carried forward to the new year. Profits left in the business to accumulate increase asset and net worth value. However, if owners' draws are greater than profits, or if losses outpace profits, net worth will decline over time, and assets will lose value as they are matched increasingly by liabilities.

profit and loss statement   *See* income statement.

profit center   A division or department that generates profits from its own activities. Departments that do not generate profits are operational centers rather than profit centers. *See* cost center.

profit-taking strategy (also called *milking strategy*)   A market approach in which the greatest possible profit is generated in as little time as possible, rather than creating longer-term product or brand loyalty and a base of customer support.

pro forma statement   A financial statement in which some or all of the information is estimated or based on a series of assumptions. For example, a pro forma income statement may be prepared as the concluding commentary on the company's current sales forecast and cost and expense budget. Business and marketing plans often summarize budgets for expansion plans and the new year with pro forma income statements.

program   Instructions developed and stored on a disk or other storage medium, which direct the computer in storage, processing, management, and output. The program repeats set routines in a logical manner, and processes information accordingly.

program evaluation and review technique (PERT)   A system for estimating the time and resource requirements of a series of tasks. PERT is often used as a monitoring device for projects. Each task or phase is broken down into a series of time-identified routines. Each is then tied together and scheduled for maximum efficiency.

projection   **1.** An estimate of future transactions, often used in reference to cash flow. The cash flow projection, when combined with the sales forecast and the cost and expense budget, is part of the comprehensive budgeting process. *See also* cash flow projection. **2.** Generally, any estimate of future transactions or levels, used interchangeably with the terms *forecast* and *budget.*

promissory note A negotiable instrument promising to pay a specified sum of money by a specified deadline. The note may also include a provision for principal and interest payments and a rate of interest and compounding method, and may be negotiable or transferrable to another person.

promotion The creation of interest in a product or service, often through a limited offer of extra value, contests, discounts, allowances, coupons, and other incentives.

property and casualty insurance Insurance providing protection against the economic losses associated with property damage or loss, and casualties or other liabilities of business property, such as acts of employees and agents, on-site conditions, and product liabilities.

pro rata liability A form of co-insurance on the same property. Two or more insurers accept a pro rata liability when the total potential loss is above the retention limit for each insurer.

prospect A potential customer or client, so designated by profile, personality, or response to a salesperson's efforts. For example, a direct salesperson may consider anyone a prospect who consents to having literature sent or who agrees to a follow-up appointment. Another salesperson may consider an individual a prospect only if he or she earns a high level of income and has net worth above a certain level.

public relations Activities undertaken to improve or maintain the customer's or the public's attitude toward the company and its products or services, to foster goodwill.

purchases journal A specialized journal used to track all purchases ordered and, later, received. The journal aids in keeping track of merchandise accounts payable and may also be coordinated with an internal requisition and back-ordering system.

pure competition A theoretical market condition in which many producers or suppliers compete for a limited amount of business, to such an extent that no one company dominates the market. Thus, the greatest output is achieved with the lowest possible price level. In practice, a market of pure competition would be rare.

Q

qualified opinion An opinion given by an external auditor as part of an audit, stating that the books and records do not completely reflect conditions that conform to generally accepted accounting principles. Examples may include interpretation of contingent liabilities, such as unsettled claims or judgments; inventory methods, valuation, or physical counts; shortcomings in internal control procedures; or treatment of transactions as part of the company's routine. The qualified opinion is given in cases where management and the auditing firm were not able to reach a compromise agreement as to the proper method of treatment or valuation; or when the auditor discovered unacceptable situations that management was unable or unwilling to alter.

qualified respondent In market sampling and analysis, an individual who meets the standards set to validate a hypothesis. The decision is often determined by personal characteristics, location, or method of approach.

> **Example:** A product test is conducted among residents of one city only. The company sets up a sample booth in the store and asks respondents a series of questions. Anyone not residing in the city is eliminated from the test as being not qualified.

quality circle A participative management technique in which a employees working in the same department or area form a team to define and solve a problem in the workplace. The quality circle appoints a facilitator and studies the problem, then makes recommendations to management. Companies using quality circles often experience impressive increases in efficiency accompanied by reductions of costs and expenses. However, it is difficult to maintain a high enthusiasm level for quality circles among employees for an extended period of time.

quality control   A system or series of systems for checking the quality that an acceptable level of quality of a product or service is maintained. The concept was first based on manufacturing and involved random checks of products at various phases of production. Applied in a broader sense, quality control may refer to administrative monitoring procedures.

quarterly compounding   Interest compounding that occurs four times per year, at the end of each quarter.

   Example: When the nominal annual interest rate is 6 percent, that translates to 1.5 percent per quarter. To calculate the annual percentage rate, (1) express the annual rate in decimal form. (2) Divide the annual rate by 4 (quarters):

$$\frac{0.06}{4} = 0.015$$

   (3) Add 1 to this quarterly rate. (4) Multiply it by itself four times:

$$1.015 \times 1.015 \times 1.015 \times 1.015 \times 1.0614$$

   This shows that when 6 percent interest is compounded quarterly, the annual percentage rate is 6.14 percent.

question and answer   **1.** A writing or advertising method in which predetermined questions are posed and then answered in a method most favorable to the product being promoted. **2.** (a) A method of presentation in which the speaker answers questions from the audience, rather than giving a prepared speech or speaking from an outline; (b) the portion of a speech in which the audience is invited to ask questions of the speaker.

quick assets ratio (also known as *acid test ratio*)   A variation of the current ratio, in which inventory is excluded. The total of current assets, without inventory, is divided by the total of current liabilities. As a general rule, the quick assets ratio should not fall below 1:1. When the ratio does fall below 1:1, it may indicate an emerging problem in controlling working capital. The quick assets ratio may be more useful than the current ratio when the company does not have inventory, or when inventory levels are stable regardless of the season.

$$\frac{A - I}{L} = R$$

A = Assets
I = Inventory
L = Liabilities
R = Quick assets ratio

quota **1.** In sales, the production goal imposed on an individual or agreed to as a matter of course. The quota may involve sales or commission dollars, numbers of cold calls, or numbers of customer contacts of all types. **2.** In statistics, the relationship between the sample and the total population, which distinguishes the degree of validity and dependability of the sample.

R

random access memory (RAM)   A type of memory in a computer that allows users to change stored information. In comparison, read only memory cannot be altered by the user.

RAM   *See* random access memory.

random event   In statistics, any event for which all of the possible outcomes have equal chances of occurring. For example, certain estimates of the future cannot be reliably based on the past. The outcome will be a random event, because there is no basis on which to evaluate the future. The solution: Monitor results as they emerge, and develop information from one outcome to another.

random sample   In statistics, a sample that provides each possible outcome an equal chance of occurring. The sample should be designed in such a way that the testing is fair and accurate; selection of test samples can build in a bias that isolates certain outcomes or prevents them from having the equal chance desired.

range   In statistics, the distance between the smallest and the largest value in a distribution of values. Range is an important issue in computing averages and in identifying the degree of dependability of a distribution. The smaller the range, the more dependable any calculation based upon statistical methods; the larger the range, the greater the degree of variance and the lower the degree of dependability and reliability of estimates. For example, in one list of seventeen values, the difference between the highest and lowest numbers is 32. In another list of seventeen values, the difference is 135. The first list is far more dependable for use as a statistical base.

rate of return   The yield, or percent return, on invested capital. In financial analysis, the rate of return may be used to compare net profits to sales or to equity. The term has a wide number of uses, depending on the circumstances and the individual using it.

rating scale   In a marketing test, respondents are asked to rate a product, on a scale of one to ten, for example. Product preference is then judged by the array of results.

ratio   Any comparison between related financial data. The ratio is a shorthand method of expressing dollars and cents, which makes analysis and reporting easier. It is easier to comprehend "two to one" than the related dollar values behind the ratio.

Percentages often are expressions of ratio values. For example, a report explains that net profit for the quarter was 7 percent of sales (net profit ratio). That is clearer than giving the dollar values and expecting the reader to calculate or perceive the percentage.

raw data   In statistics, a listing of values that has not yet been treated, arranged, or interpreted.

read only memory (ROM)   A type of memory within a computer that cannot be changed. In comparison, random access memory is a form of memory that can be changed by the user.

reader interest   The degree of interest on the part of a periodical's readership in the advertisements in the publication. The interest level is measured by the numbers interested in a particular ad (based on survey outcome).

reasonable accommodation   The conditions of the workplace and job environment that facilitate a physically challenged worker's needs successfully, without which the worker could not perform the job. A wheelchair access ramp to the personnel office is one example.

recall method   A procedure for determining the effectiveness of an advertisement by testing the respondent's ability to recall details or product names.

receipts journal (also called the *cash receipts journal* or *sales journal*)   A book of original entry designed to summarize income and cash receipts. The journal may include activity for cash sales as well as payments on accounts outstanding from previous periods.

reconciliation   The process of balancing an account by locating errors and timing differences. Errors should be corrected before the reconciliation can be considered as complete. The cash in the checking account is usually reconciled monthly to the bank statement. Some

asset and liability accounts are reconciled regularly as part of maintenance in the internal auditing or bookkeeping system.

record Logically related fields stored together within a database, with
its fields processed or developed as a single unit.

regular meeting A permanently scheduled meeting, usually held at
the same time and interval (such as every Monday at 9 a.m.). The
purpose of the regular meeting is usually limited to one or more
recurring tasks involving the meeting attendees. For example, the
project managers in an engineering firm meet each week to review
progress of active jobs. Regular meetings may also include stockholder and board of director meetings, which are required by
corporate bylaws.

reinstatement The reversal of cancellation of an insurance policy. A
lapse occurs when the insured does not make premium payments or
the policy has been cancelled by the insurer. An insurance company
may allow reinstatement within a specified time limit or under
certain conditions and restrictions. These may apply under the
theory of adverse selection. A policyholder is more likely to reinstate a lapsed policy if he or she knows of a pending claim or loss,
or if a loss is expected to be more likely in the future. The insurance
company may exclude certain losses as a condition of reinstatement,
or exclude losses occurring within the next 60 days.

release **1.** In advertising, an announcement, also called a press release,
distributed to print and broadcast media. It can announce a new
project or service or an event, or be for public relations purposes. **2.**
In law, the right or permission granted by one person to another to
use the name, product, idea, or likeness of another, in return for
consideration.

reminder advertising A brief reference offered to keep a product in
the customer's mind and to reinforce a message previously communicated. It may be visual or in the form of a phrase or song.

replacement The cancellation of an insurance policy when a new
policy takes its place. This may be done to achieve the same coverage
for lower cost, or more coverage for the same cost. The business
may also replace policies due to changes in service quality or to
improve policy conditions.

   Example: A company decides to replace its liability insurance.
The premium with a new carrier is the same, but exclusions on the

older policy are not listed; the deductible level is lower without a substantial increase in premium level; and the company's management believes the new agency will provide more responsive service.

replacement cost   A form of property and casualty insurance, in which the benefit pays the full cost of replacing lost items. Under the alternative, actual cash value, the amount paid is the replacement cost minus a computed allowance for depreciation. In many replacement cost policies, maximum benefit is limited to a percentage above the actual cash value computation.

Example: A replacement cost policy stipulates that full replacement will be paid upon loss, subject to the limitation of 400 percent of actual cash value. Machinery with current market value of $3,200 was completely destroyed in an accident. The company received "full" replacement value of only $2,800, however. The actual cash value was computed as $700 after depreciation. That value, multiplied by 400 percent, established the ceiling for full replacement cost reimbursement.

request for proposal (RFP)   A solicitation of bids on a specific project or job. A company or government agency puts out the RFP to a number of qualified contractors or other agencies, including the response deadline. Each bid is then reviewed and the job is rewarded on the basis of cost estimates.

reserve   **1.** A liability account representing the value of invested assets being held for some future use. For example, an insurance company establishes claims reserves adequate to fund future claims. **2.** A fund established from retained earnings to pay dividends or to fund capital expenditures. **3.** An adjustment to a balance sheet account, as an allowance for writing off an expense. Common examples include the reserve, or allowance, for bad debts, which reduces accounts receivable; and the allowance, or reserve, for depreciation, which reduces capital asset values and reflects depreciation expense. *See also* allowance for bad debts; bad debt; write-off. **4.** Deposits held by commercial banks in order to comply with Federal Reserve requirements.

respondent set   **1.** In research, the attitudes and attributes of a respondent in a survey toward the survey itself. These may include the attitude toward being asked to take part, answering questions, or the product itself. **2.** In statistics, the number of respondents in a promotion offer or in a survey. The number is used to judge results or the success of the promotion or survey.

retained earnings   An account in the net worth section of a corporation's books. It is the equivalent of the profit and loss account in a sole proprietorship or partnership. All net income or loss is closed into the retained earnings account and left to accumulate into the future. Offsetting the balance are distributions in the form of dividends to stockholders.

retirement plan   A program intended to provide retirement funds to an employee or self-employed person. For employees, the employer establishes the plan and funds it, either entirely or with participation from employees on a voluntary basis. Retirement plans are normally set up to defer taxes, both for contributions and for earnings within the account.

Self-employed retirement plans include the simplified employee pension–individual retirement account and Keogh plans. Individuals may also establish an individual retirement account, for which tax deductibility depends upon whether or not the person also participates in an employer-provided plan.

return on sales   Pretax, or operating, profit. To calculate, divide the net operating profit by the dollar amount of sales. Return on sales is expressed as a percentage.

$$\frac{P}{S} = R$$

P = Operating profit
S = Sales
R = Return on sales

return on stockholders' equity (ROE)   A ratio comparing net income to stockholders' equity. To calculate, subtract preferred stock dividends from net income. Divide the adjusted net income by the dollar value of common stock equity at the beginning of the year.

$$\frac{I - P}{C} = R$$

I = *Net Income*
P = *Preferred stock dividends*
C = *Common stock equity*
R = *Return on stockholders' equity*

rider   A provision added to a standard insurance policy, to provide more benefits to the insured. Examples include additional insurance, accidental death provisions, cost of living adjustments, guaranteed insurability, and waiver of premium in the event of disability.

right to work   An industrial relations concept which involves rights under law banning certain union practices, such as requiring union membership as a condition of employment. State right-to-work laws are supplemented by Section 14b of the Labor-Management Relations Act of 1947, which declares it illegal to enter into a contract requiring a union shop.

risk management   **1.** Actions and policies designed to reduce risk and the chance of loss. **2.** The auditing of existing policies and practices to ensure that an adequate level of insurance is being carried. The concept refers to any practice to reduce the incidence of claims losses or to minimize risks so that the cost of insurance will be lower. In self-insured situations, it also refers to steps taken to reduce or eliminate risk so that self-paid claims will not be excessive.

ROE   *See* return on stockholders' equity.

role-playing method   A method used in interviewing or research in which the respondent is asked to assume a role and imagine the attitudes he or she might hold in that role. It is one method of discovering the respondent's attitudes toward a product or service.

ROM   *See* read only memory.

rule of 72   A convenient formula used to calculate approximately the time required for a deposit to double at compound interest. The number of years is determined by dividing 72 by the interest rate in effect.

   Example: Money has been placed in a savings account that pays 6 percent per year. To determine how long it will take for the deposited amount to double in value, divide 72 by 6 (percent).

$$\frac{72}{6} = 12$$

It will take approximately 12 years for the value of this account to double. *See also* rule of 69.

$$\boxed{\frac{72}{i} = T}$$

i = *Interest rate*
T = *Time required to double*

rule of 69   An estimate of how long it will take for money to double when invested at compound interest. The calculation is somewhat more accurate than the rule of 72. To calculate, divide 69 by the interest rate plus 0.35. The answer is the number of years it will take to double.

   Example: Money deposited and earning 6 percent per year will double in:

$$\frac{69}{6} = 11.5 + 0.35 = 11.85 \text{ years}$$

   Under the rule of 72, the estimate of time was 12 years. The rule of 69 establishes the fact that it will take about two months less than that estimate for money to double at 6 percent interest per year.

   See rule of 72.

$$\boxed{\frac{69}{i} = D + .35 = T}$$

i = *Interest rate*
D = *Time calculation*
T = *Time required to double*

S

salary structure The range of compensation available for a specific job. Grades within the structure's range may be quite wide or narrowly focused. In some cases, the grades are expressed as codes and each grade contains a range of salary levels; each available job is then described as belonging to a grade, with a salary structure of that grade available as described in the code. Once an employee reaches the top grade in the salary structure, no further increases will be available unless granted for cost of living adjustments.

sales area test A test market in a specific geographic area where results can be obtained and used efficiently. For example, an entire sales district may be surveyed to determine how that district might do in marketing a new product or service. The sales area is well defined and distinguished from all others and can later be tracked and monitored, so that actual results can easily be compared to the test results.

sales call norm A forecast of the reasonable quota of sales calls that should be expected of the typical salesperson. It may be divided into cold calls and repeat call segments. The sales call norm can be used to measure whether newly recruited salespeople are making the effort they promised to make at the time they were hired. For example, the individual is asked to keep a record of cold calls. As long as the record shows that the minimum number of calls are being made, the agreement is kept in force.

sales incentive An inducement beyond normal compensation offered to a salesperson for achieving or surpassing a goal. Incentives may be bonuses, higher percentages of commission, prizes, or vacations.

sales meeting A meeting held for the benefit of a company's sales force. Emphasis may be on training, new product orientation.

continuing education, motivational skills, practice management, or a combination of all of these areas.

sales journal   *See* cash receipts journal.

sample   In statistics, a limited portion of a larger population, selected for study and believed to fairly represent the attributes of the entire population.

sample area   The regional limitations of a sample. *See* sample.

schedule rating   A technique for establishing rates for coverage classes on certain property and casualty insurance policies. Rates for new years are established based on actual loss experience during prior years.

scientific marketing   A marketing method in which scientific testing and statistical methods are carefully imposed on the testing method and analysis of results.

S corporation   Previously referred to as a subchapter S corporation, a corporation that is taxed as though it were operating as a small business. Profits are taxed to shareholders in a manner similar to the distribution of gains to partners in a partnership. The advantage of an S corporation is that for liability purposes, shareholders/owners are protected by the form of organization. In the event of one owner's death or retirement, the company is allowed to continue operations without disruption. In order for the election to be acceptable, only a limited number of shareholders may be involved, all must be U.S. residents and citizens, and all must agree to the election.

seasonality index   An adjustment to volume or sales, based on normal and expected seasonal variation in a product's sales. The indexing allows long-term trends to be studied without regard to seasonal factors.

seasonal variation   Changes in volume, profits, inventory levels, and other financial data due to a change in seasons. For example, in the retail clothing business, higher volume periods are associated with the end of summer and the end of the calendar year. In contracting, the spring and summer months experience gradual increases in volume, with a sudden decline after summer. For the purpose of analysis, adjustments may be made to financial results to even out seasonal factors.

secondary market A group of customers other than those thought to be the primary buyers. Secondary markets may offer the potential for increased sales or as sources for all new product or service lines.

segment **1.** A specific group of customers who share common attributes or characteristics that help the company identify methods of marketing. **2.** To subdivide a market or region for a control or marketing reason. For example, when a sales division becomes too large to manage effectively, management decides to divide it into two distinct segments.

segmentation A strategy used in marketing to isolate and market to a specific subgroup with attributes not necessarily common to the entire group. A variation might be offered regionally, in the belief that customers in that area will respond to the variation while the market at large will not.

> **Example:** A company sells pen and pencil sets across the nation. In Texas, the box containing the pen and pencil is manufactured with a star on the outside. Initial tests show that sales pick up dramatically in Texas as a result. Customers in Texas share an attribute or responsiveness to the variation.

segment reporting A section of the annual report that may be required under one of three circumstances: (1) Revenue for the segment of operations is 10 percent or more of the total for the period; (2) operating profit is 10 percent or more of combined profits for the period, before allowing for general corporate revenue and expense, interest expense, and income tax; or (3) assets identifiable for the segment are valued at 10 percent or more of combined identifiable assets.

self-employed The status of an individual or partner. Rather than acting as an employee retained by another company, the person owns his or her own company. The self-employed person is referred to as a sole proprietor or partner, and assumes all of the risks associated with owning and operating the business. The self-employed person must also provide all insurance, benefits, and retirement funding otherwise provided by the employer.

For tax purposes, the self-employed person may be an employee unless certain criteria are met. The individual must be free to set his or her own hours. The place where work is performed must be at the discretion of the self-employed person, and it harms the case if an employer/client provides an office and desk regularly. It also helps to establish self-employed status if the individual serves more than one client or customer. Most important of all, however, is the qualification that the self-employed person cannot be supervised in the same way as an employee. He or she must be independent and be allowed to work as an outside contractor.

self-insurance   Risk management without the benefit of outside insurance coverage. In some cases, a company may determine that self-insurance risks are manageable, in comparison to the cost of outside insurance and its benefits and limitations. In some cases, an employer may self-insure against losses to an extent, and provide outside insurance for high-severity losses only.

   Example: One company provides major medical through outside coverage, but medical insurance is offered as an employee benefit on a self-insured basis. In this case, the employer has determined that the cost of administering and paying limited benefits is less than the cost of group insurance.

selling expenses (also called *variable expenses)*   Expenditures that are not direct costs, but which may vary to a degree with changes in sales volume, or which are necessarily incurred to obtain sales. Examples include travel and entertainment, telephone, advertising and promotion, and related expenses. There is not a direct correlation between the expense and the sale amount; however, as sales volume increases, so will selling expenses. In comparison, there is normally a fixed relationship between costs of goods sold and sales. *See* cost of goods sold; overhead.

semiannual compounding   Interest compounding that occurs twice per year. To calculate the effective periodic rate, divide the nominal (stated) rate by 2, representing the number of periods per year.

   Example: An investment earns 8 percent, with compounding calculated semiannually. The effective periodic rate is 4 percent, so the balance will be increased by 4 percent every six months. The annual percentage rate is 8.16 percent, which is the rate paid or earned after calculating the effects of semiannual compounding. To calculate, (1) add 1 to the effective periodic rate in decimal form. (2) Multiply that by itself for the number of periods (2, with semiannual compounding):

$$1.04 \times 1.04 = 1.0816$$

(3) drop the 1. Semiannual compounding at a nominal rate of 8 percent yields an annual percentage rate of 8.16 percent.

seniority   A system for determining the order of advancement within the company or for deciding which employees are selected first for layoffs. It is based on the length of service of the employee. The concept of seniority may derive from the employer's practice or be mandated as part of a contract. It may be set in the policies and procedures of the employment manual or negotiated with a union representing the employees.

service bureau   A company that offers computer services to others on a lease or rental basis. The bureau may offer programming support, training, and set utility programs as part of its service. Charges are based on a combination of storage space, processing routine, access time, and type of routines performed by the user.

Service bureaus are good transitional choices for companies wanting to automate. The initial investment cost is low and the commitment can be made on a month-to-month basis. As long as the service bureau provides training and support, the training costs are also limited. As the system becomes more valuable to the staff, however, use will rise and costs will follow. At that point, management needs to determine whether the arrangement is still cost effective. It might be necessary to cancel the service bureau contract and automate, or to enter a period of conversion and become automated over a period of weeks or months.

severance pay   Income paid by the employer at the point of termination to help the ex-employee in the transition from one job to another. It may be paid based on a formula, such as one week's pay for every year of service, or a flat amount (two weeks; pay, one month's pay, for example). In some cases, severance benefits may be contractually stipulated. In other instances, it is given without requirement, especially when a valued employee is subject to layoff due to outside causes.

shares authorized   The number of shares of common stock a corporation is allowed to issue under terms of its articles of incorporation. Shares issued and outstanding may not reach the fully authorized share level. In cases where that level is reached, the company may amend its articles of incorporation to allow for the issuance of more shares.

shift   The time employees are required to report to work, notably in a manufacturing or production environment. Work shifts are normally eight hours or less, plus meal breaks of 45 to 60 minutes. Some shifts, considered less desirable work hours, are offered with a shift differential, inducement pay for working during evenings or midnight hours.

short-term goal   A goal with a deadline of one year or less. A goal is a specific, well-defined result that an employee, department, division, or company wants to achieve. Long-term goals generally extend beyond one year. The goal should be attainable in order for it to work, and should include a specific deadline. Employees who work from well-defined short-term goals are generally more motivated and focused than those who do not.

sick leave   Full pay for a limited number of days per year that the employee does not come to work due to illness, a benefit available to qualified employees.

   Example: A company's policy specifies that there is no sick pay provision allowed during the first three months of employment. From that point forward, the employee will be allowed up to 10 fully paid sick leave days per year.

significant variance   A variance that exceeds the budget or forecast amount by a level that is deemed significant on the basis of percentage or dollar amount, or both. Identifying and defining a "significant" variance establishes a standard for what needs to be analyzed and explained. Otherwise, it would be necessary to research and explain all variances each month, which would be excessively time-consuming and yield very little useful information.

   Example: One company has decided that in order to be considered significant, a variance must contain two attributes: First, it must be in excess of $100. Second, it must be greater or less than the budget by 10 percent or more.

simple interest   Interest that is not compounded. When simple interest is calculated, the amount never varies from one period to another, since there is no provision for earning interest on interest.

   Example: A $1,000 investment yields 8 percent per year. That investment will earn $80 per year. In comparison, compound interest increases each year as interest is calculated on the interest left on deposit with the principal. The first year's interest would be $80; the account's value would then be $1,080. So 8 percent in the second year would be $86.40 ($1,080 × 8%). Interest is compounded, so it grows each year.

See compound interest.

single-entry system   A simplified form of bookkeeping appropriate when the cash accounting system is in use and when the business has only a limited number of transactions. Each transaction is entered in the books once. The assumed offset in each case is to the cash account. Thus, cash receipts are a "plus" entry to cash and payments are a "minus" entry.

The system is undependable when the number of transactions increases, or when the books are transferred to the accrual system. Single-entry accounting does not provide the internal controls provided by the double-entry system. When the number of transactions exceeds the most minimum level, single-entry accounting should be abandoned and replaced with a double-entry system. *See* double-entry system.

sinking fund   An amount of money that is deposited over time to accumulate a target amount in the future. The amount is established assuming a specified rate of interest, compounding method, and the time required.

Example: A company wants to accumulate a fund worth $10,000 within the next three years. How much money must be deposited periodically to accumulate the target amount? The answer will depend on the interest rate and compounding method. If the deposits earn 7 percent and compounding takes place quarterly, the required quarterly deposit is $756.14. This is determined by checking a compound interest table for sinking fund factors, for 7 percent compounded quarterly. To prove the factor, consult the table below. Note that no interest is earned for the first full quarter. This is because interest credited at the end of the quarter is paid based on the previous balance.

Quarter	Deposit	Interest	Balance
1	$756.14		$ 756.14
2	756.14	$ 13.23	1,525.51

(continues)

(*continued*)

Quarter	Deposit	Interest	Balance
3	756.14	26.70	2,308.35
4	756.14	40.40	3,104.89
5	756.14	54.33	3,915.36
6	756.14	68.52	4,740.02
7	756.14	82.95	5,579.11
8	756.14	97.63	6,432.88
9	756.14	112.57	7,301.59
10	756.14	127.78	8,185.51
11	756.14	143.25	9,084.90
12	756.14	158.98	10,000.02

small business   A business employing fewer than 100 people, according to the definition provided by the U.S. Department of Commerce. A small business may also be any concern wholly owned and controlled by one family, run from a single location, or operating in only one area with limited administrative and sales personnel.

software   Programs; the series of instructions that run hardware (the operating system) or process information. In the past, software was usually developed for a single user by a programmer. This changed gradually as packaged software became widely available. Today, the trend is toward general utility software that can be used in many applications, as well as easy-to-use systems allowing an operator to tailor a system in many ways, depending on immediate needs.

sole proprietorship   An unincorporated business operated by one person. Any change in ownership (such as the sale of the business or the addition of a partner) requires that the sole proprietorship be dissolved and replaced by a new business organization. Sole proprietorships may be expanded into partnerships or the organization can be incorporated. Owners of sole proprietorships are required to file Schedule C as part of their annual federal tax return, to report business income, costs, expenses, and profit or loss. Profits are also subject to self-employment tax payable under rules of the Social Security system, which is reported as an additional tax on Form 1040-SE.

source and application of funds statement   *See* cash flow statement.

source document   A receipt, voucher, or invoice establishing the expenditure of money,. Source documents are used as verification in the bookkeeping system for expenses of a business nature. The source document is kept in the bookkeeping department's files as support for checks approved and issued. When a source document is not available, the way to document the expense is to write down a brief description, including the date, amount, business purpose, and place the money was spent. This often occurs when minor expenses are to be reimbursed from a petty cash fund, but the employee forgets to ask for a receipt.

span of control   The assumed number of people that one manager is able to manage effectively. The span of control varies with the manager, the mix of people within the department, their skill level, the location and work environment, and the history of the company and of the department.

special multiperil insurance (SMI)   A form of business liability and casualty insurance offered in a single policy, as opposed to a number of different, more specialized policies. Several coverages are available through SMI, including property content insurance, liability, crime protection, machinery losses, and other specified perils.

spreadsheet   A program consisting of a large array of columns and rows, allowing users to perform worksheet-style math routines and functions, store commands, and set up complex steps in a manageable format. The spreadsheet enables the user to establish specially tailored formats.

statement of cash flows   *See* cash flow statement.

statistical inference   The study, in isolation, of a relatively small sample of information, for the purpose of coming to conclusions about a larger population. It would be impractical in most situations to study an entire population to obtain answers. Through statistical inference, a reliable estimate may be made of the entire population.

Example: A company wishes to change the packaging on one of its products because sales volume has slacked off in recent years. To test three possible ways the packaging could be changed, the company conducts tests in limited regions, and with a limited number of respondents. From this sample, a conclusion is reached as to the best way to make the needed change.

statistics   **1.** A body of numerical information from the past, used to evaluate the present and the future. Emphasis is placed upon drawing conclusions from a limited amount of information. For example, a sample of very few people may help a company evaluate risk, estimate the future, and draw conclusions about the larger population. **2.** A form of mathematics involving the analysis and interpretation of numerical information. Statistics is tied directly to the law of large numbers: The greater the base studied, the less chance of deviation from the average and the lower the chances of error. This theory is applied in statistical sampling and testing techniques.

stock dividend   A dividend paid in additional shares of stock rather than in cash. A stock dividend may be declared by a company that is experiencing cash flow problems but does not want to omit a dividend.

   Example: One company does not want to distribute cash at the end of the quarter; however, it does want to declare a dividend to its stockholders. The board of directors declares a 10 percent stock dividend. A stockholder with 100 shares is given an additional 10 shares. The dividend is taxable as though paid in cash, even though cash was not received. This has the effect of diluting the original base of stock to a degree, since there are now 10 percent more shares on the market than before, sharing in the same net worth pool. However, because the dividend is distributed to all common stockholders equally, it is an acceptable alternative to receiving no dividend at all.

stockholder of record   The stockholder who owns shares of stock on the record date for crediting a dividend. This is a significant date since the declaration of a dividend and timing of payment will affect a large number of stockholders who actively trade in the stock. Dividends will be made only to those owners registered as of the record date. The date a dividend is declared, the date of record, and the payment date are all different. Thus, identifying the stockholders of record as of the record date is essential to keep order.

stockholders' equity   A classification in the net worth section of the balance sheet. Included in this section are capital stock, paid-in surplus, and retained earnings (in a corporation) or profit and loss (in a partnership or sole proprietorship). This combined classification represents the book value of ownership (assets less liabilities) without adjusting for any intangible assets carried on the books.

straight-line depreciation   Depreciation claimed evenly over a number of years. The same amount of write-off is deducted each year the asset is owned. The choice of this method may be through election or may be required in certain recovery periods and for certain types of assets. For example, real estate must be depreciated under the straight-line method. However, in each classification of asset, businesses are provided the choice of adopting the straight-line method even when accelerated depreciation is allowed; or of claiming depreciation on the straight-line basis, but for a longer period of years. *See* accelerated depreciation.

strategic planning   A theory of management which attempts to identify the operational environment and demands of the future, and to take steps today to anticipate and meet those demands. This may include placing crucial information in the hands of the decision makers when needed, identifying and implementing systems and procedures necessary to maintain lines of communication and information flow, and looking for the next logical step in a timely and well-controlled plan of expansion.

strike   A work stoppage organized to place pressure on management to concede to labor's demands. These may include higher pay, more benefits, settlement of a standing grievance, recognition of a union as an appropriate bargaining agent for the labor force, or improved work conditions.

subordinate   **1.** Secondary; of lower priority. When a debt is subordinated, it will be paid only after satisfaction of a senior lien or debt having first priority. In a subordination agreement, a creditor agrees to the order of priority. **2.** The relationship between employee ranks. The employees in a department are subordinates to the supervisor or manager to whom they report. Managers are subordinates to the executives or senior managers above them. This chain of command continues throughout the organization to the top, where the president and CEO (in a corporation) report to the stockholders.

subsidiary account   An account in the general ledger that breaks down a larger account into a limited degree of detail. While the general ledger should be a very summarized and simple place for reporting of transactions, some accounts can be efficiently provided with a useful degree of detail. For example, a liability account for taxes payable may be broken into subsidiary accounts for each type of payroll tax involved. This aids in reconciliation. *See* general ledger.

subsidiary ledger   An account that supports entries in other journals or in the general ledger. Subsidiary ledgers are used to break down information in greater detail than is desirable in the more summarized books and records. For example, the general ledger account may contain only a limited number of entries for accounts receivable. However, the subsidiary ledger includes transaction information for hundreds of customers. It is reconciled and balanced separately and used to generate monthly statements; and a summary of all activity is used for posting to the general ledger at the end of each month. *See* general ledger.

supplementary schedule   A schedule attached to a financial statement, tax return, or other financial report, used to provide greater detail. For example, a company shows its income statement on a single page, in very summarized form. Details making up several categories are included on supplementary schedules, including costs of goods sold, variable expenses, and general expenses. By breaking out these larger groups, the income statement is reduced to very few lines.

surety bond   A guarantee made by a company that, in the event performance does not occur as promised, the guarantor will compensate the purchaser of the bond.

sustaining advertising   A form of advertising aimed at maintaining a market for a product, through visibility and name brand identification. The purpose is to hold onto the existing market versus attempting to create and generate higher new sales levels.

swing loan   *See* bridge loan.

systematic discrimination   Practices and policies that tend to encourage, allow, or perpetuate discriminatory practices in hiring, promotion, training, and other areas. The distinctions, made on the basis of race, color, national origin, religion, sex, marital status, or disability, may even be unintentional. Systematic discrimination is not isolated, but tends to be ongoing.

T

T-account A worksheet version of an account. It is a T-shape, with debits written to the left and credits to the right. The T-account is used in reconciliation or summarizing of account analysis. It is also a useful mechanism used by accountants and bookkeepers to figure out especially complex transactions and the double entries needed to complete those entries; to reconcile accounts with many transactions; or to demonstrate to others how a particular transaction affected the books and records. The T-account is also used to train bookkeeping personnel.

tail coverage A provision in some liability insurance policies stating that the policy remains in force beyond the last date of the policy period. This protects the insured company against losses from events that occurred during the policy period.

take-home pay The amount of money a worker or employee receives after deductions have been made from gross pay. Deductions include taxes, insurance, retirement or savings contributions, union dues, and other payments or contributions subtracted from the paycheck.

tangible net worth A company's net worth, less any intangible assets. For the purpose of computing a large number of financial ratios, the distinction is an important one.

Example: The computation of book value per share requires removal of intangible assets. One company carries an asset for goodwill in the amount of $50,000. This is an intangible asset, so that amount is deducted from net worth before dividing the net amount by the number of shares outstanding.

target marketing A marketing strategy in which a specifically identified demographic or regional group is targeted and approached with product or service promotions.

Example: A financial services company has a number of products appropriate for individuals with higher than average net worth or liquidity. Most likely customers will be self-employed professionals. With this in mind, the product is target marketed to a select group of prospects.

target price A price established to create a desired rate of gross profit or return, given an assumed level of sales. For example, costs may be efficiently lowered if and when a predetermined volume level has been achieved. This may occur through better than average response to advertising, for example. If that point is achievable, then the target price will produce the desired gross margin.

task style leadership A leadership style based on the belief that working conditions, procedures, and routines work efficiently when controls are in place and work may be executed consistently. Leaders who subscribe to this style believe that the human element should be allowed to interfere with task execution as little as possible.

tax avoidance The legal planning and timing of transactions to minimize or defer income tax liabilities or to preserve current-year cash flow. Avoiding taxes can significantly reduce the liability from one year to the next.

Example: A company wants to sell its headquarters building this year and relocate to another location. Capital gains on the sale will be significant. However, instead of selling immediately, the company decides to wait three months, deferring the income tax liability until the following tax year. The motive for waiting was to avoid income taxes until the following period.

See tax evasion.

tax evasion The illegal concealment or falsification of information for the sole purpose of escaping a legal tax liability. Evasion is not the same as avoidance, which is the legal planning for reduction or elimination of liability. For example, a company that refinances a capital asset to take out the cash is avoiding taxes. Another company sells the asset but does not report the profit to the government. That is evasion, and is illegal.

tax planning The process of anticipating upcoming tax liabilities, or being aware of the tax consequences of decisions. The planning process includes modifying actions this year to reduce or defer taxes. Deferral is an important part of the tax planning process.

Example: A company invests in rental real estate. By properly planning and timing its purchases and sales, it is able to defer most of its capital gains through like-kind exchanges.

team building   A concept in organizational and management science. The theory is that, by gathering a team and discussing its goals and purposes, work performance levels are improved. The time invested in defining these matters is believed to create a common interest and build a true sense of teamwork. An important part of the team-building approach is the belief that morale, incentive, and participation levels improve when team members believe they are personally and directly involved in shaping their own work environment, and that their efforts will have an effect on the outcome.

team style leadership   A leadership theory that a motivated, committed staff working as part of a team and with a clear interest in the organization and its objective can successfully accomplish its tasks and gain an attitude of mutual trust and respect.

terminal   A machine for input to a computer system, which may consist of a typewriter-style board only, a keyboard plus a screen, or a combined input-output device including keyboard, screen, and printer.

test market   The area in which a sample is conducted. Alternate marketing plans, new products, or new labeling may be subjected to test marketing to judge possible new directions. The purpose is to identify likely market response without investing in an entire change. This reduces costs and risks.

time and motion study   A precise measurement of the time required to complete a task or a range of tasks. The purpose is to organize standards for evaluation of employee performance and productivity.

time sharing   Sharing of a large computer among several users. Time-sharing companies, often called service bureaus, allow a number of users to store and process information in a mainframe computer and to access information by means of password. Charges are based on storage space used, processing time, and routines performed. Each user develops a unique series of programs and routines, and may also access a library of uniform programs or information banks offered by the time-sharing company.

tort law   An area of law dealing with civil wrongful acts, apart from criminal acts. Torts include negligence, intentional interference, or absolute or strict liability.

total capitalization The complete capital structure of a company, which includes all sources of funding. Equity capital includes all shareholders' equity, retained earnings, and paid-in capital. Debt capital includes all bonds, notes, and contracts. The combined equity and debt capital represents total capitalization. The company may want to monitor the ratio between equity and debt capital. If that ratio moves too much toward debt capital, then profits may decline as interest expenses rise.

transaction The movement of funds or processing of information in the company. For accounting purposes, a noncash journal entry represents a transaction, even though no money changes hands. In other departments, a transaction may only occur if cash is involved. In a processing department, a transaction represents the management of one unit or execution of a routine.

treasury stock Corporate stock that was issued and later repurchased. The company may purchase its own stock when it believes that value is greater than as reflected in market value. Treasury stock may be held and later resold on the public exchange, or it may be used for internal bonuses or to pay for other companies acquired by the corporation.

trend analysis The process of analyzing financial information in order to identify and interpret a trend. The passive reporting of operations or account balances is useful, but only in a limited manner. Trend analysis interprets information, draws a conclusion about its meaning, and expresses that conclusion in the form of ratios and explanations.

trial balance A balance of all accounts undertaken as part of the closing of the books each month. The purpose is to (a) prove the general ledger is in balance before making closing entries, and (b) to set up a worksheet on which closing entries can be made.

All accounts in the general ledger are listed, with subtotals at the end of the balance sheet section (assets, liabilities, and net worth) and at the end of the income statement section (sales, direct costs, expenses). The subtotal of each section should be identical, and represents the net profit before closing adjustments.

turnkey A complete computer system, for which the user has no need to invest in any additional hardware or software.

turnover   1. In human resources, the loss and replacement of employees. Increases in the turnover rate may indicate morale and management problems. 2. In finance, (a) the estimated number of times that assets are replaced during the period, on average. A turnover analysis may be performed on accounts receivable or on inventory. (b) A ratio comparing annual sales to the company's net worth to express use of capital or capital turnover as a factor of operational efficiency.

turnover in working capital   A ratio comparing sales and working capital (the net difference between current assets and current liabilities). The ratio provides an estimate of the number of times working capital was replaced in order to produce the level of sales experienced during the year. To compute, divide sales by working capital (current assets less current liabilities). The ratio is expressed as the number of times working capital was replaced.

$$\frac{S}{W} = R$$

S = Sales
W = Working capital
R = Turnover in working capital

U

umbrella policy   A business liability insurance policy that offers protection from losses above the usual limits in other policies and provides numerous different coverages. It is more convenient than obtaining coverage from a number of carriers and tracking a number of policies.

umpire clause   A contractual provision in which both sides agree that disputes will be resolved through arbitration rather than litigation. The clause states that prior to beginning litigation, disputes will be mediated by an arbitrator or mediator acting as a neutral third party, or umpire. The provision may include the term that the umpire's findings are binding, or that upon failing to reach a mutually acceptable compromise, further steps may be undertaken, including litigation or further negotiation.

underinsurance   Descriptive of insurance policies that cover only part of a loss, meaning the business needs supplemental insurance coverage; or it may have to be self-insured. The problem may be resolved with riders, upgraded coverage, or funding of a co-insurance provision through the establishment of liability reserves.

underinsured   The condition in which a company has less insurance than it should have. Whenever an insurable economic loss would create financial consequences the company could not afford, additional insurance is needed. This is true regardless of how remote the possibility of loss. The company may have to remain underinsured when the cost of insurance would be prohibitively high.

unearned income   **1.** In taxation, investment and other income not included as "earned" income. Examples include interest, dividends, rents, and capital gains. The distinction is important for treatment of certain types of income as passive or active, as offsets against passive losses carried over from a previous year or occurring in the same year. **2.** In accounting, income received during the reporting period that will not be earned until a later period. Unearned income is reported as a deferred credit on the balance sheet, and later reversed and reported as income.

Example: A company sells the same amount of goods to a customer each month, and payment is due on the first. From time to time, payment is received before the first and the check is deposited. In those cases, it is unearned income as of month-end. The entry is made as a deferred credit, which is reversed and recognized as income during the following month.

unemployment compensation   Payment of a temporary benefit to individuals between jobs. The funds are provided by employers in the form of a payroll insurance, and disbursed by employers in the form of a payroll insurance, and disbursed by states to people terminated for reasons other than cause. Each employee is eligible for unemployment compensation based on service hours during the period prior to becoming unemployed.

unfair labor practices   Any illegal acts by unions or by management, as defined by the National Labor Relations Board. The determination that a practice is illegal may be appealed in court. However, unfair practices are also defined under terms of the Taft-Hartley Act and the Wagner Act.

unfavorable variance   A variance from a budgeted or forecast amount, such as higher expenses or lower revenues. An unfavorable variance may also occur in a cash flow projection, when additions to cash came in below expectations, or when outlays were higher than expectations. As part of the monitoring process, an unfavorable variance should be investigated immediately. Any conditions requiring greater control should be responded to with appropriate action, so that the unfavorable variance will not grow in coming months.

unilateral contract   A form of contract in which only one side promises to perform. In a bilateral contract, both sides agree to some method of performance as part of the agreement.

Example: In consideration for payment of insurance premiums by a business, the insurance company promises to reimburse losses for any covered claims. In the event of a claim for a fire or other covered loss, the contract is unilateral. The insurer promises to act by reimbursement. That action is not contingent upon any action by the insured at that point.

union shop   A company or work area of a company in which all employees are required to join a union. Any nonunion employees will be hired only if they agree to join the union within a specified period or upon qualifying for membership.

unit benefit plan   A type of retirement plan under which annual retirement benefits are calculated on a unit value. The unit usually consists of average earnings over a period of time, plus the level of salary earned during a specified period or in the latest year of employment before retirement.

unprofitable volume   A type of sales volume that does not produce net income. Unprofitable volume is characterized by excessively high direct costs or higher than expected general expenses. In either case, profits will not be realized at acceptable levels. In extreme cases, unprofitable volume will result in losses.

   Example: A company experienced a 30 percent increase in sales last quarter. However, in order to achieve this significant volume, it was necessary to offer large discounts. As a consequence, gross profit was very low. After deducting overhead expenses, the higher volume resulted in a net loss for the quarter.

update   The act of permanently changing a database, usually upon addition of new information or correction of existing files. In a batch processing system, updates consist of verifying that information is complete and in balance. Once that has been done, the batch is integrated with the permanent files and the database is updated.

user   The individual or organization using the computerized system. In an in-house system, the data processing department refers to every other department as a user, each with its distinct needs. When the system is provided by a manufacturer or consultant, the company purchasing or leasing the equipment is the user.

user friendly   An easy-to-use computer system (usually software), designed for on-line, direct communication with minimal training or outside orientation. Examples of user-friendly systems include those with menu-driven rather than command-driven routines, and simplified, logical command coding. The term implies ease of training and a quick learning curve.

V

valid contract A contract that is legal and that meets all of the legal requirements of law. Such a contract may contain no unenforceable or illegal clauses, and is entered into by parties competent to make a contract. The contract must contain equal consideration and a meeting of the minds must have occurred and exist before the contract can be valid. In addition, there must be an offer and acceptance.

Example: One company draws up a contract and mails it to another company. One provision states that, if the receiving company does not sign or otherwise respond, it will be assumed that the terms and conditions have been accepted. However, without the second party actively acknowledging and accepting the conditions, the contract cannot be made valid.

valuation method **1.** A method used to determine a covered loss for insurance purposes, used by property and casualty claims adjusters. The method may involve adjustments for depreciation based on the type of asset, its utilization, and conditions surrounding a loss. **2.** The method used by life insurance companies to establish reserve levels. That method is based on a series of actuarial assumptions concerning mortality or morbidity losses, as well as assumptions about the company's investment income. **3.** The method used to establish the value of assets in an estate, for the purpose of calculating estate taxes.

variable **1.** A type of computer field containing values that may change during program execution or processing. **2.** In statistics, a value that cannot be precisely identified or known in advance, or an outcome that might occur randomly.

variable expenses (also called *selling expenses*)   Expenses that may vary, to a degree, with the volume of sales activity. These expenses are not direct costs, since they are not part of a product or essential in order to generate sales. The level of variable expenses is also not as predictable as a direct cost.

Included as variable expenses are travel and entertainment, certain telephone expenses, meetings and conventions, transportation, advertising and promotion, and other selling-related expenses.

variance   In statistics, the degree of deviation in a distribution of values. To calculate, (1) average the squares of the values and (2) subtract the square root of the average from the result.

$$D = \left(\frac{V_1^2 + V_2^2 + \ldots + V_n^2}{n} \right) - \sqrt{\overline{x^2}}$$

D = Dispersion factor
V = Value
$\overline{x}$ = Mean
n = Number of values

venture capital   Capital invested in companies that are just beginning to operate (start-up venture capital); that are beginning new ventures or approaching new markets (expansion venture capital); or that are attempting to end a slump in markets and growth (turnaround venture capital). A company or individual with cash to invest places that capital with the company in hopes of a return on the investment. The venture capital may be in either a debt or an equity position or, in some instances, a combination of both.

Example: A venture capital company lends money to a distressed corporation. The agreement stipulates that, if the company fails to make a series of repayments, the lender acquires stock. After several missed payments, the lender would have a controlling interest in the company. This arrangement begins with debt-based venture capital, but includes a provision to convert the debt into equity.

vertical analysis   A form of reporting in which one item is assigned a base value and all others are compared to it. One well-known example is percentage reporting on income statements. Gross sales has a value of 100 percent, and all other lines on the statement are expressed as a percentage of the total. Such statements normally report both the amount and the percentage. Another application is the percentage breakdowns of balance sheet accounts. For example, total assets may represent 100 percent, and each account is reported by both amount and percentage.

Vertical analysis on the balance sheet is less valuable or meaningful than on the income statement. Balance sheet accounts are reported as of a specific date; thus, percentage divisions do not provide meaningful information. Income statement balances, in comparison, represent the sum of a period's activity. Percentage breakdown of that information is more significant.

vertical selling   Selling to customers or other buyers in a very limited range of industry, or by narrow attributes.

    Example: A manufacturer of a very prestigious line of products targets upscale consumers, such as physicians and dentists. Marketing to groups is easily achieved by selecting mail order lists by attribute, income, or profession; or by subscribers to certain magazines and periodicals.

vocational training   Training programs designed to give individuals the skills required for certain occupations or job levels. Companies may provide vocational training for employees or pay for outside training as an employee benefit. Individuals may also decide to attend a trade school as an alternative to college, where they receive vocational training to qualify for specific jobs or a range of jobs within one industry.

voidable contract   A contract that may remain in force, but which may be cancelled at the option of one of the parties. A defrauded party to a contract may elect to keep the contract in force even with evidence of fraud. A minor who has entered into a contract may elect to declare the contract void or keep it in force.

voting stock   All shares in the corporation that give voting and proxy rights to the current owners.

W

wage incentive   A motivation based on pay, usually aimed at achieving higher productivity, lower defect or error rates, or faster output. The incentive is based on a measurable factor and often is expressed and practiced as a contest among shifts or individuals. In order for the incentive program to work, the employee must have a clear and precise understanding of (a) the expected level of performance and result, and (b) the reward.

waiver   A clause in an insurance policy which excludes certain types of losses or limits the degree of reimbursement that will be offered for certain types of claims.

   Example: The manufacturer of dangerous materials may receive a waiver in a property and casualty policy excluding any losses resulting from exposure to those materials, or from fires caused by ignition of the materials.

weighted average   The average between two rates, when one side carries a greater degree of weight than the other.

   Example: Your company is making payments on two separate loans. The outstanding amounts are different, as are the interest rates. You have been asked to calculate the interest rate on the total debt. To do so, calculate the weighted average. If the first loan has a balance of $41,000 and involves interest at 11.5 percent, and the second has a balance of $22,000 and interest of 8.75 percent, what is the weighted average? To compute, (1) add together the outstanding principle balances; (2) calculate the weighted interest for each and add the rates together:

$$(41/63 \times 11.5\%) + (22/63 \times 8.75\%) = WA$$

$$(0.65079 \times 0.115) + (0.34921 \times 0.0875) = WA$$

$$0.0748 + 0.0306 = 0.1054 \ (10.54\%)$$

$$\left(\frac{P_1}{PT} x\,r\right) + \left(\frac{P_2}{PT} x\,r\right) = W$$

P_1 = Principal, first loan r = Rate of interest
P_2 = Principal, second loan W = Weighted average
PT = Principal total

window A viewing area within a larger computerized routine. The term is often used to describe the relatively small portion of a spreadsheet in view on a terminal screen at any one time. That window is the area in which the user is able to work; it may be moved or adjusted so that the window shifts to a new area.

word processing Manipulating and managing text in a computer program. Letters, memos, contracts, reports, and other business text may all be stored in files within a word processing system. The information can be updated, moved around, edited, and otherwise changed before an upgraded version is printed out. Or, output similar in form or content to other files already in the system can be quickly and easily reproduced.

workers' compensation Payment to employees for sickness or injury arising from conditions of employment or the work environment. The employer incurs a liability for workers' compensation with or without negligence. Benefits include hospitalization and medical care, as well as compensation for loss of income.

    Medical benefits are divided into two types. Under coverage A, an insurance company agrees to pay all of the compensation and benefits required by the state workers' compensation laws. Under coverage B, a commercial insurance policy is provided as a supplement for losses not covered under workers' compensation laws.

working capital The amount of net funds available to pay for current operating expenses. Working capital is the difference between current assets and current liabilities. This value is used in a number of balance sheet ratios, as well as in trend analysis aimed at monitoring management effectiveness in controlling and providing operating cash flow.

worldwide coverage   A form of expanded business liability insurance providing for coverage even when losses occur overseas. Certain forms provide the coverage but limit the amount of loss that will be allowed.

write-off   **1.** Recognition of a loss in the books of the company, or an expense being booked during the current fiscal and tax year.

>   **Example:** A corporation has been carrying an account receivable for many months. The customer is not going to be able to pay the bill. At the appropriate time, this is recognized as a bad debt, and the asset (account receivable) is written off. Many high-volume companies manage such write-offs by setting up a reserve and booking bad debts periodically; and then modifying the rate of write-off based on actual experience over time.

>   *See also* allowance for bad debts; bad debt; reserve.

>   **2.** Any transaction that provides a tax benefit to the company; an item that can deducted on a tax return.

>   **Example:** A company is considering investing in real estate. In comparing costs and benefits, one worthy consideration is the range of write-offs available, including interest, taxes, maintenance, and depreciation.

Z

zero–base budgeting (ZBB)   A method of budgeting in which all requested budget items must be fully explained and documented, preferably based on a series of logical assumptions. Thus, when variances do occur, they can be explained intelligently. The ZBB method is endorsed in many companies, since it requires a constant evaluation of budgeted levels. In the alternative, explanation may be required only for items that exceed the previous year's spendings. Therefore, if one year's spendings were excessive, that excess is built into all future-year allocations. Zero-base budgeting eliminates this problem.